Basketball: Coaching for Success

A Philosophy of Basketball and the Drills to Implement it

By Bob Hill

Foreword by Bill Fitch

COACHES ≡ CHOICE™

SPORTSMASTERS

ISBN: 1-58382-004-3
Library of Congress Catalog Card Number: 99-60464

Cover Design: Britt Johnson
Front Cover Photo: ©NBA Photos, Mitchell Layton
Diagrams: Janet Wahlfeldt and Michelle Summers
Page Design: Michelle Summers

a **SPORTS**MASTERS book, published by Coaches Choice
Coaches Choice Books is a division of   Sagamore Publishing, Inc.
P.O. Box 467
Champaign, IL 61824-0647
Web Site: http://www.sagamorepub.com

Dedication

This book is dedicated to Richie Buckalew of Atlanta, Georgia. Richie currently works as a scout for the Atlanta Hawks of the National Basketball Association (NBA) and formerly served as a scout for the New York Knicks. He was instrumental in my receiving my first appointment in the NBA as an assistant coach for the Knicks.

Those of us who know Richie and his wonderful family have benefited greatly by his example as a good husband, father, basketball player, and coach.

The courage with which Richie handles life's challenges continues to inspire me and all those who know him.

Acknowledgments

I have many people to thank, since this is my first book, and I have spent the past 32 years in college and professional basketball.

My wife, Pam, and our three sons, Cameron, Chris, and Casey, have provided constant support.

My writing coach, Jan Kilby, has guided me in writing this book.

Tom Newell, Bruce O'Neal, and others at the United States Basketball Academy encouraged me to write this book.

Hubert "Hubie" Brown, Larry Brown, Tim Grgurich, Pat Haley, and Ted Owens, head coaches whom I served as an assistant coach, taught me so much.

Richie Adubato, John Calipari, and Doug Collins have engaged in hours of debate with me over literally everything about basketball.

Howard Garfinkel has always included me in basketball camps conducted at the Five Star Camp in Pittsburgh, Pennsylvania.

Bill Walton has shared hundreds of basketball experiences with me and many others attending the Pro Development Camp.

Jojo White has answered hundreds of my questions regarding his playing days with the Boston Celtics.

John Anderson, David Craig, Lenny Currier, and Mike Saunders have been trainers who have worked overtime to keep players on the court.

The San Antonio Spurs who have always desired to become a team, and their loyal fans have my greatest appreciation.

My assistant coaches, Ed Badger, Dave Cowens, Brad Greenberg, George Irvine, Brendan Malone, Bobby Ociepka, Paul Pressey, and Randy Wittman, have all been loyal and hardworking.

Many head coaches of various NBA teams have required that I work diligently as a coach and continue to learn. They include Chuck Daly, Mike Donleavy, Cotton Fitzsimmons, Chris Ford, Mike Fratello, Del Harris, Dick Harter, Phil Jackson, George Karl, Jim Lyman, Dick Motta, Don Nelson, Pat Riley, Jerry Sloan, Rudy Tomjanovich, and Lenny Wilkins.

My coaching friends have shared their thoughts with me throughout the years. They include Billy Bayno, Dave Bliss, Herb Brown, Mike Brown, Ken Burmeister, Randolph Carroll, Gordy Chiesa, James "Bruiser" Flint, Bob Fox, Larry Hogan, Rex Hughes, Frank Martin, Bob Murphy, Bill O'Connor, Dave Pendergraft, Dave Pritchett, and Andy Young.

Michael Goldberg, my first agent, also needs to be thanked.

Finally, I thank Bill Fitch for being my coach and friend.

Contents

Foreword

What are the chances of a college coach recruiting a high school basketball player to his college program, coaching him, and then, years later, coaching against him in the National Basketball Association? The chances would range from slim to slimmer, or, to use one of my favorite sayings, be about as rare as a nudist with a good memory for faces.

In spite of the odds, this has happened to me twice in my coaching career. Naturally, I am very proud of both of my former players and the careers they have carved for themselves. The first was Phil Jackson, a modern legend among coaches with his six NBA championships with the Chicago Bulls. The second of my young recruits to coach against me in the NBA was Bob Hill, the author of the book you are about to read and a successful coach with a winning record accumulated with the Knicks, Pacers, and Spurs. I recruited Bob out of Worthington, Ohio, to Bowling Green State University, where he excelled in baseball and basketball, just as Jackson had done at the University of North Dakota.

Bob Hill has been a student of the game of basketball from the first time I met him over 30 years ago. His teams have been well coached in the fundamentals of the game and have exuded an interest in game preparation, and he has always seemed to be on the same page as a team, which, in this day and age, is a real credit to a coach. When you consider the teams Bob Hill has coached, the many other successful coaches whom he has served, and his worldwide experiences, you instinctively say, "Bob should write a book." He has written a fine book, putting his philosophy and principles of teaching and coaching on the printed page.

Bob has written a comprehensive book, full of anecdotes, figures, and lessons to be learned from his many experiences. This book can be a great guide for young coaches just starting their careers, as well as for veteran coaches who want to incorporate new ideas and methods into what they are now doing. Fans of basketball will also enjoy reading this book.

by Bill Fitch

Introduction

When my father hammered my first basketball goal onto the front of our garage years ago, I never imagined spending my life in the game. I was simply interested in shooting the ball up to the rim. My interest in basketball grew quickly, however, and developed into a passion in the years following that first shot that probably did not even hit the rim.

Now, as I look back at the life in basketball that I have truly enjoyed, I am motivated to share the many lessons I have learned. I hope that sharing them will influence readers in a positive way.

The integrity of the game of basketball has always been of the utmost importance to me. The best coaches and players help to preserve the integrity of the game. I define integrity as complete personal honesty and responsibility.

Throughout the years of basketball's glorious history, many changes have occurred. These have included such technical changes as eliminating the center jump following each made field goal, widening the lanes, and adding a three-point shot. Adapting to technical changes is the responsibility of both coaches and players.

Changes involving players have also been instituted. In years past, most players came to the game of basketball with a respect for coaches, team members, and the game. Because some of today's players seem to need to learn such respect, coaches have greater team-building challenges. To assure a team's success, coaches must increasingly not only help their players to develop their basketball skills, but also their human relations skills.

Developing a philosophy about each aspect of the game is essential to effective coaching. Becoming a student of the game can enhance one's effectiveness as a coach, teacher, or leader. Embracing growth as a goal can enable coaches to adapt to further changes within the profession.

Coaches must work to become complete coaches—not merely defensive coaches, offensive coaches, or players' coaches. A complete coach understands that a successful team can best be developed through a balanced approach to coaching players to excel both defensively and offensively. A successful team's performance usually reflects such an approach.

The purpose of this book is to share my experiences through a holistic approach to coaching. I hope to challenge the thinking of coaches, players, and basketball enthusiasts about many of the aspects of the profession—aspects that I believe are essential to success. I also hope to inspire all the participants in a basketball program to grow both personally and professionally.

Chapter 1
A Philosophy of Basketball Coaching

Developing a Coaching Philosophy

Philosophy: a system of ideas based on experienced thinking

The philosophy of a basketball coach probably first begins to take shape when he becomes intensely involved as a player. Once a player becomes a coach, he often does not even realize he has a philosophy until he begins to discuss his views on the subject. His philosophy then continues to develop as he experiences various aspects of the sport.

As a coach's career continues, it is vital for him to have a mental blueprint of how a team should play—and why. Committed players will only adopt a coach's approach to a game when they understand his philosophy behind it.

A coach must be able to respond to his players' questions about strategies for success. A team's core leaders must support their coach's philosophy for the coach and the team to be successful.

My Philosophy of Basketball Coaching

My philosophy of basketball coaching began in the mid-1960s, when I played high school basketball. My philosophy developed further as I played college basketball, coached college basketball teams for 14 years, coached an international team for one year, and coached National Basketball Association teams for 13 years.

My ideas are the result of many experiences with some outstanding coaches and even more outstanding players. My experiences with less talented, yet determined, athletes have been just as rewarding.

The Nature of the Game of Basketball

Basketball was invented to be played at a quick pace. Anything done at a quick pace is subject to error, and anything subject to error is unpredictable. Therefore, basketball is an unpredictable game. A coach's job is to eliminate unpredictability without interfering with his players' innate ability to play.

Three Coaching Goals

Basketball coaches should approach their job with three goals in mind: (1) creating a positive environment, (2) teaching fundamentals, and (3) team building.

Creating a Positive Environment

Establishing an environment for a team that is efficient, supportive, and distraction-free becomes essential if coaches want player commitment. To help build this environment, coaches and players should arrive early for practice. Promptness helps to ensure that players can complete their work well.

The equipment manager, the trainer, and the assistant coaches should all be available to players prior to practice sessions. By being available, they demonstrate a supportive attitude that most players appreciate.

Creating professional relationships can also produce feelings of support. Being available to support the continual growth of individual players and the team can help ensure a professional approach to the game and also help a team to reach its potential.

Coaches can eliminate distractions by allowing only players, coaches, trainers, and equipment managers to attend practice. Such sessions should be dedicated to team improvement and preparation. Players and coaches should connect through high levels of concentrated work in a private setting.

Teaching Fundamentals

Teaching the proper fundamentals involves demonstrating them and working hard individually with players and then progressing to two-on-two, three-on-three, and ultimately four-on-four. With each stage of teaching, a learning curve can be charted. Each progression takes time to develop. Time must be managed, and drills must be well planned and precise. Repetition leads to proper execution.

Initially, players execute drills in the absence of defenders until they display the proper footwork skills. Adding defenders comes next, at which point players often revert to their old ways.

Coaches must be firm but patient. Players eventually become skilled enough to move forward.

Learning occurs in each stage of development, and it finally consists of coaches teaching players five-on-five, helping them with their offensive and defensive skills, and pointing out strategies for special situations. Eliminating a long learning curve becomes a coach's ultimate goal, but the coach must understand that learning takes time. The process starts over when coaches begin working with the entire team.

Daily repetition becomes important. Drills must be consistent with one's coaching philosophy, or the process will never end.

Team Building

An ongoing process, team building becomes as important as teaching fundamentals, if the objective is to eliminate the unpredictability of a team's performance. The true test of a coach's ability as a leader lies in his ability to build successfully a team.

Coaches must daily provide high levels of inspiration. They achieve this goal through their philosophy, drills, personality, work habits, organization, preparation, and energy level. A coach must set the pace daily for staff and players. Players define themselves when coaches provide inspired leadership; in the process, they assure a coach that they are dependable.

Motivation comes in many shapes and sizes. Motivation leads to a team's reaching its potential and helping its members achieve something positive during a season. It is vital that the entire team share the vision of the coach and his staff for the next season or two.

The coach must then give his vision a structure with regard to how to fulfill his team's destiny. Creating realistic goals, as well as action plans to accomplish those goals, provides that structure. Players must know what they are trying to accomplish and where they are in the process.

Having a vision and an action plan gives a coach a theme for motivational speeches. If the players support their coach's philosophy and style of play, they will learn how to handle winning streaks and stop losing when a slump occurs.

Just as important to success in basketball is a balanced approach to coaching. Effective coaches know that defense keeps teams from losing, offense helps them win, and the middle of the floor can make or break them at any time. Coaches must teach their players to succeed at the defensive end, the offensive end, the middle of the floor, the sidelines, the baseline, with both clocks, and to create consistent rotation for a team. Such strategies lead to balance in a team's performance.

Players appreciate a coach's desire to help them enjoy success. The challenge lies in teaching players where their responsibilities begin and end. Developing teamwork that encourages players to feel ownership for their team is the last step. They will then accept their responsibilities and feel accountable for the results.

Elements of Balanced Coaching

A balanced approach to coaching can be achieved by understanding the following seven principles: (1) defense keeps a team from losing; (2) offense helps a team win; (3) the middle of the floor must be played; (4) game preparation can eliminate surprises; (5) players must be coached to anticipate special situations; (6)

clocks must be managed to help a team gain extra possessions and the last shot; and (7) rotations intended to get players their minutes can promote player accountability.

Defense Keeps a Team from Losing

If the goal is to become the best team in the league or to lay a winning foundation for the future, defense becomes the cornerstone. Playing great defense, though, does not guarantee success. A team also must move forward so it can score at the other end.

Great defense can, however, help keep a team in position to succeed. Defensive basketball remains a team concept. All five players have certain responsibilities. All players, in spite of their ability to play individual defense, can become effective team players.

Coaches must recognize a team's strengths defensively and use them wisely in a particular system. Once players understand a team's defense and learn to adapt to it, generating stops becomes both challenging and enjoyable.

Playing defense as a team allows players to change momentum, create surprises, force action, and catch up when necessary. When players achieve stops as a team, it creates the existence of what all successful teams share: a willingness to play basketball together.

Offense Helps a Team to Win

Most players want to play at the offensive end of the floor. They want their shots, and they want as many minutes of playing time as possible.

Offensive pressure ensures a high-quality offense. Pushing the ball after a block, a steal, a rebound, a made field goal, or a made free throw allows a team to make an easy basket. Such pressure also tests an opponent's ability to play transition defense, as well as its conditioning and depth. Offensive pressure gives players who are not great shooters the opportunity to score and feel that they are a part of the entire game. Ultimately, offensive prowess can build team harmony.

Transition offense must be executed with the purpose of placing players in a position on the floor where they can be successful. Spacing on the floor throughout the actual transition and using the width of the floor at the end of transition can contribute to a team's success.

Some coaches create a system with movement, such as the passing game or the flex, which calls for movement with more structure. Others believe in continuity offenses that can create three or four options for scoring attempts. Other coaches prefer that players use more quick-hitting plays to allow shooters to take more shots. The fact that people coach the game in different ways makes it challenging.

The Middle of the Floor Must Be Played

Converting from defense to offense means utilizing the middle portion of the court. Such special situations as out-of-bounds plays can occur in the middle of the court. Spreading out an offense and playing keep-away while protecting a lead utilizes the middle of the court. Developing a half-court trap will force both teams to use the middle of the court. Players must understand that the corners at half-court can be utilized defensively.

Conversely, in offensive play, team members are wise to keep the ball away from the corners to eliminate traps that can create problems. Using the half-court line properly against certain defenses becomes necessary. Coaches simply must teach both offensively and defensively the situations that are bound to occur from the three-point line to the three-point line.

Game Preparation Can Eliminate Surprises

Many veteran coaches believe that preparing for a game can be as important as winning. Some even believe that preparing is more important than winning, because without preparation, the team will never achieve its potential as a team.

Since game preparation remains so essential for success, coaches must make it part of their philosophy and that of their players. Preparation, however, takes time. Opponents should be scouted before playing a game, and scouting reports should be prepared for the coaching staff. Watching game tapes can increase a coach's knowledge of an opponent's tendencies.

Studying the opposing coach's approach to handling special situations can certainly be helpful. Studying how teams catch up when they fall behind, or how they protect game leads, can also be helpful.

Pre-game walk-throughs need to be well planned. Long walk-throughs can overload players and, as a result, become counterproductive. Pre-game talks to players regarding the coach's game plan should be concise and include only essential points.

Players Must Anticipate Special Situations

Coaching and teaching players to anticipate special situations can help assure that a team will have the opportunity to react properly while under pressure. Whether players execute a two-for-one situation at the end of a quarter, a half, or a game, or whether they can handle a surprise trap following an out-of-bounds play, they need to handle these situations well. Chapter 5, "A Philosophy of Handling Special Situations," provides greater detail on why developing players' skills in such special situations becomes vital to a team's success.

Clocks Must Be Managed

When coaches spend time in practice teaching players how to manage both the game clock and the 24-second clock, teams often become more able to maintain leads and win games. Since basketball is regulated by time, players need to take advantage of it.

Teams need to have out-of-bounds plans that can produce the shots needed from anywhere around the court, regardless of the time remaining. Even desperation shots may work well if players have practiced making them. Valparaiso University proved this point during the National Collegiate Athletic Association (NCAA) tournament in 1998. The winning play was executed so well that the shot produced was a great, well-balanced shot.

Having as a team goal the ability to master the clock situations can pay dividends.

Player Rotations Can Promote Accountability

Having a plan for the regular rotation of players into the game at specific times according to the clock can lead to success. This strategy works well for a variety of reasons.

Team members perform best when they know when they will play. They then have more time to prepare effectively. They also look forward to their minutes so they can play well. When players know they can play through their mistakes, they become more productive. Most important, players become motivated and accountable when they know their minutes will be extended if they play extremely well, and reduced if they do not.

Coaches need to prepare a schedule of rotations in case of foul problems or injuries. Many times, players who are not in the regular rotation schedule can still be helpful in special situations.

How I Developed My Philosophy

High School Basketball

As a basketball player at Worthington High School in Worthington, Ohio, from 1963 to 1967, I was fortunate to have two excellent coaches, Bernie Weiss and George Kliene. Both men had a passion to coach. They were also honest and instilled discipline every day. As a result, our team became competitive.

Both coaches wanted to succeed, but they never compromised their values to do so. They taught us about developing enduring values that would make us professionals.

The team came first, and team rules were enforced. Prior to my sophomore season, our best player became involved with the police after committing a prank.

He was dismissed from the team. As a sophomore, I was greatly influenced by this incident because of my admiration for the player. I had always felt great respect for Coach Weiss, but felt even more respect for him afterward.

George Kliene became my coach our senior year. He had high standards from which he never deviated. Our team played together at both ends of the floor. George was the first coach who seriously influenced my thinking about the game. He taught us the value of being a complete team so that we had a chance to succeed at either end of the floor. His philosophy helped our team finish with the best record in school history. The record still stands today.

College Basketball

Bill Fitch, when he was at Bowling Green State University (BGSU) in Ohio, recruited me to play basketball in 1967. He would later become a Basketball Hall of Fame coach.

He taught us so much about basketball that I could write an entire chapter just on him. His first lesson focused on the importance of conditioning. He taught us that, oftentimes, conditioning would make the difference between success and failure. Bill Fitch always looked people in the eye and told them the truth. He was honest.

In addition, Bill taught me that practice time was an invaluable part of each day and that our performance would be a direct reflection of our practice habits. During practice, he expected a great deal from us and from himself. Our sessions were all business.

Bill became the second coach in my playing career to emphasize playing both ends of the floor. He also made sure to teach all of us that discipline would always play a major role in successful basketball.

College Coaching

Following my college playing days, I was given the opportunity in 1971 to begin my coaching career at an early age. Pat Haley, head coach at BGSU, hired me as an assistant coach. He thought I had potential to become an effective coach. I worked as an assistant coach while completing my master's degree in secondary education. At that time, one needed a graduate degree to coach at the college level.

Having been a basketball player for so long, I thought at first that coaching would be simple. Being thrown into coaching at an early age, however, soon felt scary. When young coaches work from a position of fear, they work diligently.

The first lesson I learned from Pat Haley at BGSU was to teach players to succeed at both ends of the floor. Second, I learned that a coach can only succeed through organizational skills. Third, I learned the obvious importance of managing time and developing the capacity to work and make any sacrifice necessary to succeed. (My early years in coaching were full of mistakes, but I tried not to make the same mistake twice.)

Finally, I learned from Pat how important loyalty is to the success of a college program. All head coaches are public figures who receive both praise and criticism. Working with a head coach should be looked upon as an honor by an assistant coach.

After four years at BGSU, I moved on in 1975 to the University of Pittsburgh as an assistant coach to Tim Grgurich. Tim had been a longtime assistant coach at the University of Pittsburgh before becoming head coach. He was loyal to his family, to the basketball program, and to the university. To say we were workaholics would be an immense understatement.

Beyond learning the value of work, I was able to observe a coach who was totally committed to his existence as a coach. Tim served as a walking inspiration—on a daily basis—to everyone who worked for him and played for him.

Tim's other assistant coach, Fran Webster, had developed the "amoeba defense." Tim was a defensive-minded coach, and our teams were a reflection of his personality. With Fran and his philosophy of defense, our team developed excellent skills at one end of the court and average skills at the other. We scored many points, however, as a result of our defensive skills. My growth as a coach was enormous during the time I spent with Tim and Fran.

Ted Owens then hired me in 1977 at the University of Kansas in Lawrence. Dr. James Naismith had been the first coach at Kansas and the only losing coach in the history of the KU program. Basketball was life in Lawrence, and it was a real honor to be a part of the program.

Coach Owens is a good man, and his players enjoyed playing for him. He conducted excellent practices with an emphasis on fundamentals at both ends of the court. Footwork was important in our practices, both offensively and defensively. Ted was the third coach in my career who felt being competent at both ends of the floor was essential. At the time, Ted was the second most successful coach in Kansas history, after Phog Allen.

Before I worked with Ted, he had taken his teams to the Final Four on two occasions and to a number of Big Eight Championships. He had high standards and treated people with respect. He was honest with people. In spite of his success, he always had time for others.

Larry Brown, who became my next boss at the University of Kansas, brought another dimension to my development. Larry strongly believes in teaching fundamentals at both ends of the floor. He places enormous emphasis on defense and offense, but he also emphasizes team play. He believes strongly in players sacrificing for their team.

Larry was the first coach I ever heard speak constantly about players caring about one another to make each other better. At the core of Larry's coaching lies a deep desire to have his team members play together all over the court, and they did. Stressing team play on a day-to-day basis became part of my coaching philosophy.

Coaching in the National Basketball Association

In 1985, I began coaching in the NBA as an assistant to Hubie Brown, head coach of the New York Knicks. By then, I had learned some important lessons and developed some values in my philosophy as a coach. Hubie was a defense-minded coach. He believed firmly in discipline and structure and would be confrontational with the players if they drifted from his control. With his involvement in statistical work during games, along with his solid preparation for both practices and games, Hubie was ahead of his time. His outstanding work ethic, his love for the game, and his passion for coaching were unparalleled.

I could not have begun coaching in the NBA with a better coach than Hubie Brown. After he left the team, I became the head coach.

We are all products of our past experiences, that teach us lessons that define our growth. I was fortunate as a player and as an assistant coach to know some outstanding head coaches who helped develop my philosophy of coaching. I enjoyed observing different qualities in each coach and adopting them in my role as a coach.

Throughout my 15 years of working as an assistant coach, I encountered some coaches who spoke only about the value of defense or the value of scoring points. Some seemed to have respect for only one end of the floor or the other. Now, having spent 14 years in professional basketball, where I have had to be concerned about all of the factors that contribute to a team's success, I find that my philosophy has changed: Teams must play both ends of the floor, because defense keeps teams from losing and offense helps them win.

Chapter 2

A Philosophy of Success

The Importance of Teamwork in Life and in Basketball

Every basketball player comes to a team with different levels of experience and skill in being a part of a team. Coaches, too, have different levels of experience and skill as team members.

My early years were extremely influential in my learning the value of teamwork. I grew up an only child of wonderful parents. My mother was a beautician who had her beauty shop in the front room of our home. My dad managed a restaurant in the back of our home. We lived in the middle.

I had daily chores to do in both the beauty shop and the restaurant. Before school and after school, I had to complete my chores. At night, before dinner, we would count the day's earnings and prepare the money to take it to the bank.

Early on, I was a team member, though I did not realize it then. The dynamics of teamwork that I learned shaped my personality. Every day was an experience in commitment, responsibility, sacrifice, honesty, and trust. These values became important values in my life. Only later, when I realized all of the lessons that I had learned, did I appreciate my formative years.

Not everyone today values teamwork. Some do not understand its importance, and others simply do not have time for it. Perhaps I became interested in coaching because of the lessons I had learned early in life. As it turns out, team building determines the success of coaches and, ultimately, their teams.

When I think of team building, I always remember the time I spent in 1993 and 1994 as assistant coach of the NBA's Orlando Magic. NBA teams are managed a variety of ways and bought for a variety of reasons. The goal of each franchise—a multimillion-dollar corporation—is principle-centered leadership.

The night before our opening game in Miami, the organization had a kickoff party for players and coaches and their wives. At the end of the evening, Rich DeVoss, the team's owner, arrived and asked to speak to the team.

Rich showed that he clearly understands the value of teamwork. He spoke to the team for 30 minutes about the seven ingredients of success. He made it clear that he cared about each person. He told them they would be "America's team."

His talk was unbelievably effective. Though he never mentioned winning, it was clear he thought the team would win. By spending time with that young team, he set the stage for the season. The players all understood that he cared about them and supported them. He gave the entire team an identity.

Throughout my career in basketball, the landscape has changed. Today, the need to develop players' human relations remains a great challenge. Because not all players arrive with respect for coaches or the game, coaches must spend time developing unity within a team, as well as on teaching fundamentals.

My philosophy of success now seems like a gift given to me by my parents, by the coaches with whom I have worked, and certainly by the many players I have coached. I have learned that a team that develops a high level of self-esteem can overcome barriers and shatter records. Ingraining this self-esteem in his players should be an important goal for every coach.

Traits of Successful Teams

Several traits are essential in order for basketball teams to be successful. In Figure 1, I have outlined those I consider important.

Commitment

Commitment: entrusting all of one's skills mentally physically, and spiritually to a good cause

Before coaches can expect their players to make a commitment to the team, the coaches themselves must make that same commitment. They can begin by demonstrating a work ethic that inspires players day after day. Coaches should plan all aspects of a team's activities and consistently communicate those plans to their players. They should always provide their players with what they need, whether it is praise, suggestions for improvement, or discipline. Coaches should also prepare players in advance of a season for everything that may occur.

Ultimately, coaches must create an environment in which players enjoy working. Coaches who commit themselves to the growth and success of their players become successful coaches.

To help their players increase their commitment, coaches must first know each player's level of commitment. Players today can be classified in one of three ways: committed, cooperative, or dissident. Coaches would be happy if all players were either committed or cooperative. There are players, however, who feel compelled to challenge authority and the integrity of the game. In many cases, dissident players

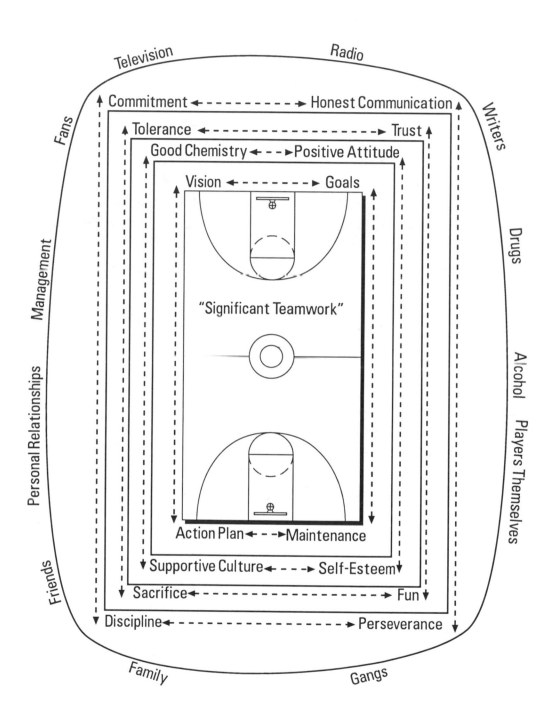

Figure 1: Traits of Successful Teams

can be cut from a team, suspended, terminated, or traded. In some situations, however, a talented, but dissident player cannot be terminated. Coaches must then do something positive with a negative influence.

One solution coaches can use is to become more diligent and committed, if possible. Through sincerity and hard work, coaches can increase the desire of all of their players to give back to the team and, consequently, to provide the team with the ability to succeed. The goal is for cooperative players to become committed and for dissident players to become at least cooperative. Players committed to a team from the beginning expect coaches to be equally committed. Such players become a team's best role models and recruiters. Their loyalty, however, begins with commitment by the coach.

I had the opportunity to work with a committed player while coaching the Indiana Pacers. Detlef Schrempf was committed to the team, to success, and to professionalism. I asked him to make many changes throughout our experience together. He always made the changes and then made the changes work for the team.

Playing big forward came naturally to him. I moved him to the small forward position to allow Dale Davis to play big forward. I later asked Detlef to come off the bench to be our sixth player, and the NBA subsequently named Detlef Sixth Man of the Year. Detlef makes commitment part of his existence as a player.

When I think of committed players, I also think of Avery Johnson, a player with whom I worked when I served as head coach of the San Antonio Spurs between 1994 and 1997. Avery approached me on our first flight to Nashville, Tennessee, for an exhibition game against the New York Knicks. He asked if I minded if he watched game tapes with me on our flights to games. I could hardly believe my point guard wanted to watch game tapes with me.

For two seasons, Avery and I, along with the assistant coaches, watched game tapes. The experience was rewarding. We accomplished so much on every flight. Avery and I ultimately developed a relationship that carried over directly onto the court. He and I were not only on the same page, but we were also side by side in the same sentence. This opportunity helped me to empower my point guard—something our team needed desperately. Avery Johnson's total commitment spilled over to his teammates every day.

Honest Communication

Honest communication: not only telling the truth as one knows it, but also sharing past experiences that may contribute to the cause

The process of team building requires that the coach be honest with his players. Once players feel secure in the knowledge that their coach is honest, the coach can then demand the same in return. Through consistent honesty, coaches can avoid resentment that can eventually sabotage a team.

Coaches who can communicate honestly with their players usually are also able to acknowledge their deficiencies. They feel accountable for their responsibilities. Creating honest relationships allows coaches to accept their responsibilities and to expect players to assume theirs as well.

Honesty can help lead to the development of other qualities necessary for good teamwork. Once team members feel the impact of truth, they feel comfortable being themselves, and their talent flourishes.

Teams in professional sports work together every day for seven to nine months. During this time, they become well acquainted. Sometimes they help each other with personal problems, if they trust one another.

An incident revealing the importance of honesty between coaches and players occurred while I coached the Indiana Pacers. Early one season, the team had played well, but there was ample room for improvement. We were on the road the afternoon prior to a game one night.

As I watched tape in my hotel room, someone knocked on my door. It was Vern Fleming. Vern was a veteran player who always played well and cared deeply about succeeding. He said he had some concerns he needed to talk about. As he talked, Vern expressed concern that a new player brought in the previous spring through a trade was tearing our team apart. Vern wanted something done about it. I had been doubtful of the player's level of commitment but had been trying to help him succeed.

As time went on, I realized Vern had been right. We were able, however, to manage the situation and make it to the playoffs. Vern's honesty allowed our team to reach our goal of returning to the playoffs.

When I think of honest communication, I also remember an incident that involved David Robinson of the San Antonio Spurs. Early one season, we were on a flight to Minneapolis to play the Minnesota Timberwolves. Avery Johnson and I were watching a tape as David Robinson walked back to ask if we could talk. I said, "Absolutely," and David and I moved back a few rows to have some privacy.

David expressed concern about one of the players on the team. Once we had finished our conversation, David, a born-again Christian, began sharing some ideas about his beliefs. His belief in the Lord lies in the center of his life. David's personality changes when he talks about his strong beliefs. He becomes animated, wearing his belief all over his body.

I decided to take a chance and ask him a question that no one had ever been able to answer for me. I told David my father had been a wonderful man, one of my heroes, but that I had never understood why the Lord had taken him at the young age of 62. I told David I had even met on three occasions with my minister, who seemed unable to help me.

David explained for 40 minutes why the Lord had taken my father. I felt better, and, perhaps, I wanted to feel better because it was David doing the explaining.

As the plane landed, David seemed to have resolved his concerns about the player, and I felt more at peace about the loss of my father. I'll always remember that flight. We had engaged in truly honest communication.

Discipline

Discipline: creating a behavior pattern

With the proper amount of discipline, coaches always have a chance to succeed. Without it, they never do.

Too much discipline can stifle a team's innate ability to play. Not enough allows the players to deceive themselves.

Therefore, it becomes necessary to establish disciplinary standards, along with rules, to help the players meet those standards. Such standards must be fair, and they should be established for the appropriate reasons. Rules must apply to everyone associated with the team—not simply the players.

The most important aspect of discipline, however, is its enforcement. To avoid enforcing established rules shows a lack of honesty and commitment to the success of the players, the staff, the trainers, the equipment managers, the management, and, eventually, the fans.

Team building always presents challenges. Without the enforcement of rules to control the behavior pattern of those in a program, coaches eventually fail. Coaches, as leaders, must be accountable for the enforcement of rules, even if it means losing a game or two or three. There are no shortcuts to creating a foundation for success.

Coaches' values will be severely tested. If they surrender their values, they will lose the respect of the committed players and, eventually, the remainder of the team. If coaches develop a set of values, they must make sure that they endure.

Having a dissident player presents a challenge. Having a dissident player who happens to be especially gifted presents an even greater challenge.

Managers or owners of professional teams, as well as athletic administrators in college sports programs, must be careful not to expect coaches to compromise their values by overlooking rule violations by talented, yet spoiled and dissident, players. Winning a game does not ensure a team's success. Only when coaches remain true to their values will the necessary solid foundation be established.

Perseverance

Perseverance: to remain constant in one's dedication to a purpose, idea, or task in spite of obstacles

By instilling in his players the values of commitment, honesty, and discipline, a coach should be well on the road to developing an effective, successful team

©NBA Photos, Bill Baptist

Coaches must also persevere. The ability to develop enduring values determines who becomes a leader. At the same time, the willingness to listen to differing viewpoints also becomes necessary.

In the world of sports, many athletes persevere so they can reach lifelong dreams and goals. Coaches who work with such athletes should learn from them.

A number of years ago, Brian Scanlan was a 6'7" walk-on at Bowling Green. He did not possess great athletic ability in basketball. He made the freshman team and earned time on the court simply because of his diligence.

The summer after his freshman year, Brian hitchhiked his way all over the country, going from basketball camp to basketball camp. He challenged better players to play one-on-one and learned all he could.

Brian returned his sophomore year a different player. He earned a starting position on the varsity team and seemed to improve with each game.

After the following two seasons, Brian spent his summers working and playing at camps. Prior to his senior season, the team had greatly improved its skills. Brian assured the coaching staff that he would come off the bench in order to help the staff and the team.

Brian helped Bowling Green to reach postseason play for the first time in years.

Following his senior year, Brian joined a tour of players going to Europe. They hoped to sign contracts with European teams. He later left the tour, signing a contract in Brest, France, on his own. For the next 13 years, Brian played professional basketball in Brest.

After moving back to the States for good, he invested his savings in a chain of beach wear stores in Florida. Today, Brian Scanlan is a millionaire who still lives in Florida. His perseverance in the game of basketball allowed him to create a life for himself and his family.

Players demonstrate their lack of perseverance when they arrive late to practice, to the team bus, or to appointments with trainers. They sometimes then try to negotiate with coaches regarding penalties. In the NBA, for example, such players may ask coaches if they can pay a fine instead of being prohibited from playing in a game. In such situations, coaches must enforce their rules and communicate to their players that they do not need their money, but rather, their compliance with the rules that help build a successful team.

Tolerance

Tolerance: putting aside differences for the betterment of the cause

Members of sports teams rarely all like each other. Teams usually have cliques, and these cliques, can become barriers to team building. Coaches cannot allow players' differences with others to harm a team's performance. Therefore, coaches should encourage players to demonstrate tolerance. Coaches who procrastinate in addressing this issue may find that their players' intolerance spreads and may eventually destroy their team.

Promoting the value of tolerance among players may be easy, difficult, or impossible to do, but it remains important. If a commitment to honesty, discipline, and perseverance exists in a team's environment, a coach's task will be made less difficult, because his players will feel a responsibility to be tolerant.

Coaches, as leaders, must address this issue. Stressing the value of tolerance to team members serves as a beginning. If players remain intolerant, individual meetings must follow. In certain cases, the only recourse may be to have players who have conflicts with each other meet to discuss the problem. Reducing players' minutes within games usually solves the problem, if other efforts fail.

One strategy coaches can use is to encourage team members who dislike other players to communicate with them on a professional basis for the welfare of the team. Coaches can encourage such players to engage a disliked player in game-related discussions and other activities. This step often helps to restore professional relationships among players and also to reduce personal conflicts.

This strategy can be extremely important when the disliked player is a dissident player. The strategy can be even more important when the dissident player also happens to be a great player.

Trust

Trust: firm reliance

Trust allows sports programs to prosper. Trust develops as a result of commitment, honest communication, discipline, perseverance, and tolerance. Within each team-building process, each quality leads to the next. Thus, teams become more powerful as they develop over time.

As in all leadership scenarios, trust begins with coaches themselves. Players must learn that they can trust their coach in every way. Once players know coaches are trustworthy, they are inclined to trust one another.

In basketball, trust becomes an emotional investment by team members and coaching staffs. Trust determines whether a team will succeed or fail.

In every walk of life, trust remains a key ingredient to significant success. With a sufficiently talented team, one can win games without generating high levels of trust. If, however, a coach's vision is to have the best team, trust must be developed. Trust starts and ends with the coaches.

As I have discussed, honest communication and perseverance serve as cornerstones in developing significant teamwork. They are also key elements in developing trust with players. In professional sports, this process is more difficult because some players feel they have been lied to in contract negotiations with owners or have been shown some other form of disrespect. Thus, they do not trust coaches.

Other NBA players, however, feel that the NBA treats them fairly. Such players more willingly trust coaches.

Coach-player relationships have changed from what they once were. In earlier times, players developed trusting attitudes as youngsters.

Building trust always takes honesty, perseverance, integrity, and inspiration. Today, even when these qualities already exist in relationships, there are no guarantees.

Coaches must be aware of the importance of trust. Their players must learn quickly that the coaches have a commitment to them and can be trusted completely.

One experience I had taught me the importance of a players being able to trust his coach. When I coached the San Antonio Spurs, we were once on an eastern trip that started in Detroit. The trip was late in the season, so we were working diligently to put the finishing touches on a great regular season.

About 5:30 or six o'clock in the morning, I was asleep when someone knocked firmly on my door. I woke up concerned that something was wrong with a player. I jumped out of bed, ran to the door, and asked who it was.

The voice from the other side of the door belonged to David Robinson. I opened the door to see David dressed in a Nike running suit, with his Bible in his hand.

After he stopped laughing at how I looked, he assured me that everything was fine with him, his family, and the team. He said he just needed to spend some time with me.

David sat down. He began by explaining that he, Avery Johnson, and Sean Elliott had studied the Bible the previous night. They'd had a great session, and all had benefited from it.

He then said that later that night he felt the Lord sending him the revelation that he should become the dominant player in the league. He wanted to discuss the remainder of our schedule and game strategies.

I enjoyed hearing him talk that way, sounding so involved in the team. Following a 30-minute conversation, he returned to his room.

We continued to succeed. David played extremely well and was ultimately named the league's Most Valuable Player.

David is a special person who has sound values based on his Christianity. Our conversation was a special experience in which I felt he trusted me with a matter as private as his personal goals.

Sacrifice

Sacrifice: giving up something of value for the sake of the team

Once players make an important emotional investment in their teams, they become willing to sacrifice. Making sacrifices throughout a season becomes mandatory and solidifies the trust generated by team members.

Players who love the game know that sacrifices are part of their responsibility to give back to a team. They continue their efforts, whether or not their team succeeds. Many cooperative and dissident players are unable to maintain this view.

Maintaining accountability is easy when a team succeeds. The ultimate test comes in the face of adversity. Players clearly reveal themselves in the midst of conflict. The desire of players to make necessary sacrifices can quickly diminish, so coaches must be prepared to address this issue.

Sacrifices come in many ways. Consistent, effective defensive rotations that end in physical confrontations with opponents remain one popular form of sacrifice. In such situations, coaches often say, "The player really sacrificed his body."

Players who think "pass first and shoot second" know the meaning of sacrifice. Veteran players who take extra time to develop the skills of younger players during practice also understand sacrifice. Such players often sacrifice out of their appreciation for the efforts of their teammates.

Fun

Fun: enjoyment, pleasure, or amusement

Allowing fun to be part of a team's experience has always been part of my philosophy. Throughout the long season, fun can be the perfect remedy for a problem. When teams enjoy success, having fun can be a form of reward. The celebration of small victories should be an integral part of creating team confidence.

Properly managing fun, however, is also important. A team must understand why the coach has decided to use a little fun to break up the action. Fun should have a purpose, and players should have the proper attitude while enjoying a fun activity.

In 1996, the Spurs were enjoying a successful season, and I felt that the team deserved some appreciation other than an occasional accolade from the staff. One particular practice was scheduled two days prior to a game. I felt we could win if we continued to play the way we had been playing. Team members were taped up and then warmed up as usual. Following our shooting period, I had the players line up on the baseline. I announced that practice would be over for the day if David Robinson could walk on his hands to the free-throw line.

The immediate positive response from David's teammates who showed their support of his efforts was impressive. David had no problem reaching the foul line, so he continued to half-court with his team members walking alongside him, encouraging him the entire way. There was a celebration at half-court before they returned to the locker room.

Everyone enjoyed this activity, and the team appreciated the time off. By that time, they all understood that I trusted that practice the following day would be go well, and it did, and we continued to succeed.

Good Chemistry

Good chemistry: an effective blending of the composition of personalities on a team

People often say a team has "good chemistry." If only the process of developing chemistry were as simple as it appears. Despite a team's ability to achieve high levels of character and commitment to success, achieving harmony can be a delicate process.

Coaches, like orchestra leaders, must work on blending the talents of those they lead with each performance. If the environment in which a team works includes the ingredients mentioned so far in this chapter, maintaining harmony becomes easier, although it sill remains challenging.

Basketball remains an emotional experience that has the constant potential for emotional eruptions. The more significant the game, the greater the potential for such problems. Effective leaders always provide solutions in time to prevent a team from losing. The ability of coaches to communicate honestly often becomes tested during such heated moments.

At times, no one person can solve the problem, so a team simply needs a cleansing session for everyone to be honest with everyone else. The exercise I'm going to describe has always worked. All players, coaches, trainers, strength coaches, and managers must participate in the session.

The rules are simple. The team sits in a large circle so everyone can look at everyone else. When a person is being addressed, he must be quiet and listen.

In the first round, each player says what he appreciates about each person in the circle. After everyone has finished, the group should take a short break.

During the second round, each player says what he does not appreciate about everyone in the circle. Again, each person must be quiet while he is being addressed.

When everyone has finished, the coach can allow general discussion. By the end of the session, everyone has expressed his complaints and feels better about himself and about the team.

This process promotes honest communication. Players, coaches, trainers, and equipment managers sitting in a circle learn to become honest with one another. Honest communication is necessary for success.

A Positive Attitude

A positive attitude: a hopeful, encouraging outlook

The majority of life's lessons reveal that attitude determines the success or failure of most people. Unfortunately, coaches do not always have a team whose players have positive attitudes. Therefore, a plan to help develop such attitudes becomes necessary.

Developing proper team attitudes often requires a strong commitment from team leaders. When teams do not possess such leaders, the responsibility rests solely with their coaches and their staff. All of the ways in which coaches allow teams to function help to determine team members' attitudes.

Coaches should praise the efforts of players possessing positive attitudes. Developing a team's attitude, a constant responsibility of coaches, can lead to their developing confidence. Success depends on confidence. Breakthrough experiences in basketball result from positive attitudes.

Coaching Avery Johnson of the San Antonio Spurs was enjoyable in many regards because he was a committed player with a phenomenal attitude. Before playing for the Spurs, Avery had played in the NBA for years, but had never had a chance to establish himself. I'm sure there were times during his career when he had experienced disappointment, but I doubt that he had ever become discouraged.

Avery's enormous determination was fueled by his exemplary attitude. Avery doesn't possess a great jump shot, nor does he have much range. Going to his right can sometimes be an adventure.

Because of his size, Avery has trouble defending his opponent at times. (Keep in mind that I'm describing my starting point guard on a team that averaged 60 wins for two seasons.) Avery succeeded because he was given the opportunity to play for the Spurs, he was empowered by his coach, and he had a positive attitude. Avery's motivation focuses not just on winning, but beyond. He works diligently year round to play as well as he can. At the end of his playing days, he will be able to look back and honestly say, "I did the best I could."

A Supportive Culture

A supportive culture: one that brings out the best in both an individual and a group

The efforts of the players generally establish a team's culture. Coaches might be inclined to say, of course, that such a culture needs to be focused on success.

Perhaps the culture of world-championship teams focuses on success. Coaches of such teams understand success intellectually and are able to teach teams valuable lessons. More importantly, such coaches feel secure enough in their role to allow team leaders to develop a culture of success.

Whatever the source may be, teams do, on occasion, have the ability to embrace a certain intellectual aspect of their existence. As long as the culture developed stimulates positive growth, it can help the overall success of a team.

Players who attempt to gain control of teams through self-serving activities, however, must be stopped in their efforts to influence a team's culture. Effective team leaders should be allowed to influence other players. All other influences need to be monitored by coaches.

The Spurs have a spiritually oriented-culture, and the players have been solely responsible for its development. Their culture motivates them to succeed.

Prior to taking the floor during our first exhibition game in Nashville, Tennessee, in 1994, I asked the players to stand in a circle and hold hands for a moment of silence. This was something I had done for a long time, so I didn't think much about it.

As we bowed our heads, David Robinson started to give a prayer. He had not prepared it; he simply spoke from his heart. When he was finished, everyone said, "Amen."

That was the first time a player had ever offered a prayer during my team's moment of silence. I had no idea then that David's prayer in Nashville would start something that became vitally important to the Spurs' success over the next two seasons.

Following the game, I returned to my hotel room to watch the game tape. I realized then that the team's three born-again Christians—Avery Johnson, Terry Cummings, and David Robinson—may have especially appreciated that moment of silence. Both Avery and Terry had preached, and David considered himself a teacher of Christianity.

Prior to the next game, Avery gave the pregame prayer, with Terry giving his prayer prior to game three. From that point forward, the three players rotated the responsibility of leading prayers.

As this process continued, the prayers that each player gave became more thought out. Avery would find excerpts from the Bible that paralleled the task we had at hand. His prayers became a significant part of the entire process. As the competitive spirit of David and Terry took hold, they, too, began to put more effort into preparing their prayers.

This prayer ritual became important to the team. Everyone looked forward to the prayer, and it became a major part of what the team was all about.

During my second season, Charles Smith and Monty Williams joined our team at the All-Star break. Although no one was aware that both players were born-again Christians when they arrived, it was not long before this fact became obvious.

Following a few pregame prayers, Charles Smith asked David's permission to join in the rotation of players who were offering prayers. David replied, "I'll have to discuss it with Avery and let you know."

David and Avery decided to give Charles the opportunity he sought, except during significant games. Charles accepted their decision and gave some prayers, though not consistently. As the coach, I only learned about this arrangement well after the fact.

Certainly, a player's saying a prayer does not guarantee success. With the Spurs, however, this ritual became an important part of their approach to each game. They developed the team's culture all on their own.

Self-esteem

Self-esteem: a feeling produced by one's image of himself and fueled by success

A team's ability to win the games it should win can generate confidence. Once the players raise the bar by winning games they could lose, they begin to develop self-esteem.

Giving teams new, reachable challenges remains a leader's responsibility. A team's ability to meet such challenges can help lead it to breakthrough performances that establish levels of self-esteem never before felt.

Such experiences help teams lay a foundation for future success because they reward the dedication of the players and the coaching staff. They often involve learning lessons that need to be learned.

Basketball players and coaches often learn lessons that parallel those experienced by people in all walks of life. Because these lessons are valuable, learning them is always worth the effort.

With a young and inexperienced team, any success can be extremely important. Whatever a team's stage of development, the players should develop as much confidence in themselves as possible. In the process, coaches should point out why their players are succeeding at any particular moment, and they should also keep their focus on the important aspects of their players' development. If coaches take success or failure for granted, their teams will reflect their poor attitude.

Once a team develops a high level of confidence, the players should know which games represent their breakthrough games. Such games determine a team's growth and success. For example, defeating an opponent that a team has not defeated in a long time or succeeding on the road in a facility in which a team has never won before are challenges for which coaches should prepare their teams.

Along the way, it is helpful in building confidence to celebrate small victories, but also to keep celebrations in perspective. When a team succeeds through excellent performance, a coach should lead the celebration, assuring players that the victory reflects the way they are capable of playing. A coach can also point out individual performances that led to the team's success. Players should learn to take pride in themselves and in the team, but only for displayed ability.

During my first year with the Spurs in San Antonio, we experienced a rocky start. Some players had experienced injuries, but overall we simply had not played well. The team's confidence wavered. I knew we were going to succeed, but I just wasn't sure when.

We arrived in Houston to play the Rockets, reigning NBA champions from the year before. Being in such close proximity to Houston, the Spurs felt a sense of rivalry with the Rockets. Winning the game became a major goal for us for several reasons.

My pregame talk that night was all about where we were at that point in the season and what we had to do to be where we wanted to go. I challenged the players for 30 minutes, and I also assured them we could succeed. I tried my best to give them confidence and backed up my statements with schedules and statistics all over the board.

Since we had not played well up to that game, we had nothing to draw from to give us the kind of confidence needed to succeed in the Summit, the Rockets' home court. We had to believe in ourselves and play well together to obtain the much-needed victory.

We somehow found confidence early in the game. We won the game and gained even more confidence. We retained our confidence for the remainder of the season. Our record from that game forward proved to be the best in the league that year and the best in franchise history, as we finished the regular season 62-20.

In the process of accomplishing our goals, however, we still had breakthrough games that needed to be won to be eligible for the playoffs. Another team that stood in our way was Seattle. The Spurs' history of winning games on the road in Seattle had been terrible. We again had to succeed in a game on the road, something we had not been in the habit of doing.

At that time, however, we were playing well and had high levels of confidence. The team knew we could succeed if we defended, rebounded, and scored off of excellent defensive work.

The night of the game, the game tape played in the locker room, the board was full of information, and I reviewed my pregame talk as players watched the tape. (Seattle had defeated us soundly in the first game of our series at home.) As I walked to the back of the players' locker room, I could tell that the players were focused. I thought my speech and my review of the board went well. We were ready to go, I thought.

The players formed a circle and held hands as we always did in preparation for the team prayer. Avery Johnson began the prayer by moving forward into the circle a step or so. He squeezed his eyes shut as he began to deliver his important prayer. He had obviously prepared for this moment and didn't want to make a mistake. He spoke about a devastating hurricane that had swept through and left no survivors. He said everyone and everything in the way of the hurricane had been destroyed. Avery then spoke about our team's destroying teams in our path and said Seattle was next. When he finished and we all said, "Amen," the players erupted in a celebration as though they knew they were going to succeed in that important breakthrough game.

We had an outstanding performance and won the game. The players had always been confident, but they soon developed a level of self-esteem they had never experienced before.

Developing self-esteem requires character. In addition, the players on the team must adopt their coach's philosophy. In the case of the Spurs, a culture had been established. The players' beliefs helped to move us a step closer to believing we could reach our potential.

From Traits to Success

Vision

Vision: unusual foresight

Coaches spend time prior to assuming a new coaching position by dreaming about what could be. They dream this again as they approach each new season. Having vision is important. What is more important is having a plan to make one's vision clear.

Developing a philosophy of success is critical. Such a blueprint gives a coach something to implement while moving forward with a team through the season.

Only through teamwork can the players on a team progress toward a vision. As players begin to embrace the power of selflessness on the court, their coach's vision becomes clearer.

Goals

Goals: the finish line

Along with vision, goals become necessary. If players know their weekly goals, they have incentives.

Coaches create goals in accordance with their vision. Players should provide input in order to feel accountable. One of the major challenges in professional basketball is defining players' responsibilities. Players who feel a sense of ownership about a team naturally embrace their responsibilities and feel the effects of success and failure.

Action Plan

Action plan: a proposal to do something

When a vision has been created and goals established, an action plan must be developed. Players need to learn from coaches how they will reach their goals.

On a daily basis, players must know where a team is in regard to reaching its goals. For example, the NBA plays 82 games over a six-month period, so there are many ways to divide a season into groups of games. Coaches can analyze season goals on a monthly or weekly basis, classify games as home versus road, or establish groups of 10 games.

However a coach decides to analyze a season, players must become aware of not only the team's past record, but also where it is within a certain segment of the season. Part of every pregame talk should include where a team is and what it must do to accomplish its goals for certain groups of games.

Some players do not realize where their team is in the standings or even who their next opponent may be. Most coaches look ahead in order to keep themselves organized. Players do not always do so, so a coach must help them learn to do this.

Along with explaining where a team is within each group of games, coaches should have players look at league standings every day. The best place to post such statistics is on a door or a wall that the players see as they enter their locker room. Another way to keep the players informed is to talk to them during pre-practice meetings.

Maintenance

Maintenance: to preserve or retain

Team building is a daily process. A coaching staff must be aware of the importance of maintenance and be on the alert to solve minor problems whenever possible.

Team captains and team leaders must also try to respond appropriately to comments in the locker room that can become poisonous and demoralize a team. Everyone must be committed to preserving what has already been established.

Coaches, especially, must not procrastinate. As soon as they become aware of a problem, they should deal with it.

I have used two methods to help preserve team harmony. One method works well during daily stretching periods, when the players always form a circle. I walk around the inside of the circle and communicate with each player. In this way, I am able to learn a great deal about the mood of the team, and, besides, the players appreciate the attention.

The other method is to meet with the captains and team leaders once or twice a month, whether the team does well or poorly. A coach's desire to keep a team together through wins and losses is a sign of consistency that players appreciate.

Distractions

Distractions: whatever diverts a team's attention

Distractions in many forms appear every year at every level of basketball. When coaches create an environment in which teams can practice, they want it to be distraction free. Practice may be the only time coaches have their team to themselves, besides seeing all of the players in the locker room prior to games and after practices and games.

Some distractions are unavoidable. The media have a job to do, and it is the job of coaches and players to cooperate with them. Team owners have every right to address anyone they please. Families and friends are an integral part of every player's life. Beyond these normal distractions, however, other issues, such as alcohol, drugs, personal-relationship problems, and late-night parties, can also become distractions.

A distraction of any kind can become an opponent to a team and its efforts to succeed. If players become a team, however, they will have the strength to defeat these opponents.

Dealing with distractions remains a goal as important as any other goal. Unfortunately, distractions can become major issues throughout an entire season.

Coaches must ultimately assume responsibility for helping to protect players in certain situations. They have to be committed to the team.

Chapter 3

A Philosophy of Defense

Defense keeps teams from losing. Defense must fuel a team's offense

Within a balanced philosophy of coaching, it is essential to understand that the defensive end of the floor must consistently serve as the grass roots of a team's performance. Since a team has no ball when playing defense, its success largely depends on all five players working together.

Dissecting a well-executed offensive play exposes two- and three-person games. Defensively, a team must use all five players to counteract the offense. Creating this perception of a five-man effort among the defense is essential.

A coaching staff must create a defensive blueprint that begins and ends with three ingredients. Having a commitment comes first. This process, established by the coaching staff, must be a major part of a playbook's practice plans, as well as a coach's pregame talks and walk-throughs, game plans, and postgame evaluations.

The second ingredient, developing absolute trust among players within a defensive execution, becomes a team's source of confidence and aggressiveness. If one breaks down the development through part-method teaching (as opposed to the whole-method approach of coaching five-on-five), drills can become an avenue of trust. Players will learn their responsibilities and grow in their desire to help one another. The best defensive teams not only look forward to helping each other, but also to helping helpers. When all five defenders have a single-minded approach, the defense is grounded and ready to be tested.

The final ingredient to developing a successful defense is concentration. A team's ability to execute its defensive game plan is born from its collective concentration. Players who have a clear understanding of a coach's rules concentrate easily. How quickly they learn to execute a defensive game plan under pressure for an entire game remains the responsibility of the staff and the players.

Defensive Organization

Coaches must develop a philosophy of defense. In order to teach and coach such a philosophy successfully, however, coaches must organize the learning process. How coaches analyze the court should be a product of their personality and beliefs.

I learned years ago to analyze the court numerically. Throughout my experience, numbers have remained important. I have, however, added colors and lines to my figures. Psychologists suggest that people retain more of what they see than what they hear. As such, players should see a court in order to learn how to analyze it.

Numbers conveniently indicate where the ball should be picked up and pressured by the defense. A full-court defense, labeled a 40 series, indicates full-court pickup. A second number indicates a specific defensive strategy (i.e., straight man, run-and-trap, run-and-jump, or zone). The 30 series begins at the three-quarter court, the 20 series begins at half-court, and the 10 series begins at the three-point line.

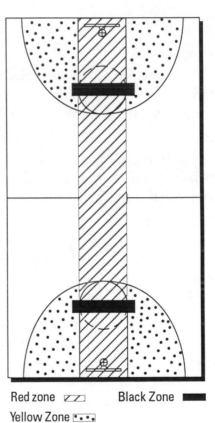

Colors also send a message to most people. Seeing specific colors within a defensive court diagram allows players to visualize their defensive responsibilities. Using a figure with a red zone in the middle of the floor shows players the area of the floor in which no balls should be allowed. This area creates a number of problems for a defense. For example, it provides the ball handler with four convenient receivers, it permits a straight angle to the basket, and players shoot the ball at a higher percentage in front of the goal. In addition, a defense can collapse, forcing tall players off the board and giving

Red zone ▨   Black Zone ▬

Yellow Zone ⋯

Figure 2: The Defensive Court

an opponent offensive rebounding opportunities. Finally, it opens up the possibility of three-point shot attempts.

A yellow zone around the basket represents an area of ball pressure in which a defensive team must push the ball toward the sideline. The goal becomes pressuring the ball at the three-point line and keeping it away from the red zone. Rotations should occur across the red zone into the yellow zone. When properly executed, these moves force opponents to play on the sides of the court—and this increases a defensive team's chances for success.

A black zone extended from elbow to elbow represents an area in which players should cut off the court and eliminate a passing lane to the red zone. Most offensive plays have options that include entry passes from the foul line and higher to the weak side of the floor. A defensive team wants to pressure passers so that they are forced to move back to the strong side of the floor. This move allows weak side defenders enough time to do their jobs and, in some cases, challenge the three-second rule. Allowing a player to make a quick reversal pass or a penetrating pass for an easy basket cannot be tolerated.

Defensive Goals

Defensive goals are necessary but must also be well planned. Such goals must be reachable, and there is no sense in having too many. Too often, goals set by a coach do not affect his team's performance, but rather are established to promote and justify certain outcomes. Whatever their goals, coaches should make them represent the essential elements of a defensive plan. Every player and coach must understand the purpose of a goal and how it correlates to success.

The first consideration of a coach when establishing defensive goals should be the offensive style of his team. If a coach advocates walking the ball up the court to use up time on both the game clock and the shot clock, fewer points will be allowed by his defense. Of course, the number of points his team scores will also be lower.

Many coaches associate this style of play with the defensive end of the floor, but this is not the case. Playing a slow, deliberate style of basketball never guarantees high-quality defense—only lower numbers.

If a coach's offensive style consists of having players move the ball fast, looking for a quick shot with no regard to the clocks, point totals rise. If a coach's offensive style consists of having players move the ball with a definite purpose while probing for easy baskets, a team's scores will be somewhere in the middle of the scores obtained by using the other two styles.

No matter what one's offensive philosophy, the most important goal to establish is the differential—the number that separates the points allowed and the points scored. The differential remains the basis for establishing meaningful defensive goals.

Since a sound defense will keep a team from losing, the coach must plan goals with this thought in mind. Creating a differential goal means creating proper balance in a team's performance. Although the final differential will be established at season's end, creating game-to-game goals is essential.

Reducing an opponent's field-goal percentage also becomes essential. The exact percentage desired should be established by the staff and the players. The reason the players should be so involved is that their involvement in creating goals will increase their accountability. Helping to determine what the goal should be in reducing an opponent's shooting percentage gives players more of an incentive than they might otherwise have.

Two game goals help prompt a defense to reduce its opponent's shooting percentage: (1) contesting shots and (2) providing helps. Contesting occurs when a defensive player either moves one of his hands up and around a shooter's wrist, thus creating an adjusted shot, or rotates quickly with his hand up so that he rushes the opponent's shot. Contesting 50 percent of an opponent's shots will reduce that team's field-goal percentage.

Helps occur when a player either rotates below dribble penetration, thus forcing a pass, or rotates to stop dribble penetration, causing the offensive player to turn the ball over or take a poor shot. Forcing an opponent to take jump shots also will reduce that team's shooting percentage. The more helps a player makes, the more pressure he adds to a team's perimeter defense. Players who pride themselves on providing helps should begin to take more pride in guarding their opponents.

Keeping statistics on players' helps during a game should help to promote team play. Another advantage of keeping such statistics is that it helps to identify those players who are constantly helping their teammates. Such players should be rewarded for their efforts. Staff should also record the number of help situations that were not executed. It is probably best for an assistant coach to assume responsibility for keeping track of helps.

While continuing to reach the ultimate goal of a differential, players should strive to score points off of their effective defensive play. Creating turnovers helps to position a team to score.

Another way to help establish a differential is to deflect the ball. Deflections occur when a player either places his hand on the ball, deflects a pass, blocks a shot, or tips a dribble. The goal of achieving deflections encourages active feet and active hands and ultimately results in better pressure. Although six to eight deflections a quarter or 12 to 16 a half is a reachable goal, the coaches and the players should establish the exact number they deem desirable. Deflections can produce turnovers, and turnovers can produce points. Consequently, a team should be given an incentive to reach the ultimate goal of establishing a differential.

Two more ways to score points through effective defensive play are to rebound aggressively at the defensive end of the floor and go after loose balls. Both of these strategies need to be priorities.

Defensive rebounding is essential. Succeeding on the defensive boards demands a team effort. Each player should feel responsible for rebounding. In most games, the guards can help considerably simply by obtaining the long rebounds and loose balls. High-quality rebounding places a team in a position to create easy basket opportunities and reduce an opponent's field-goal attempts. Effective defensive rebounding also eliminates free throws produced by a great offensive rebounder.

Many coaches try to keep records of rebounds from the bench. Setting a goal for all players to go to the board 90 percent of the time they are on the floor, however, can be a better approach. A coach should give the responsibility for recording rebounding to two people other than assistant coaches. One person should be responsible for the guards, while the other person should be responsible for the front line.

Each player should be graded on the number of times he attempts to go to the board during the game. For example, if a small starting forward plays during a period in which 20 shots are taken by the opponent, the forward must go to the defensive board at least 18 times, which is 90 percent of the time. Notifying players of their percentage after each game can increase their activity on the defensive board.

A defensive team can also score points through an effort to control loose balls—the intangibles of the game. Guards are usually in the best position on the floor to see loose balls, so they should assume responsibility for obtaining their share. All players, however, should assume this responsibility. Obtaining more loose balls with each game should become a goal. The staff responsible for recording players' rebounding statistics can also record players' success in controlling loose balls.

It is essential that a team set realistic and reachable goals that are consistent with a specific coaching philosophy. These are the goals that determine success. These are the goals that should always be embraced by the players.

Drill Philosophy Terminology

Coaches should avoid conducting drills simply because they like them. Nor should they plan to conduct too many different drills in any one practice session. Instead, they should conduct progressive defensive drills that are part of a plan. Such drills should be consistent with the coach's rules and philosophy.

Drills should always be competitive. Players who achieve success during these drills should be rewarded, which should give them more confidence. The losers should have to pay a price—running at the conclusion of practice.

Because players need to react to the possession of the ball and also sprint with space and purpose, drills should be conducted on the full court. By using the entire court, the coach can also give his team work on transition defense and help it achieve the goal of creating proper balance in the team's overall performance.

Defensive Drills

Transition Defense

Until the rules change, transition exists as the first line of defense. Maintaining defensive balance within one's offense is always a priority. Transition is the first aspect of high-quality transition defense and another example of proper balance between offense and defense.

Basketball, a game of action and reaction, requires all team members to be aware of who possesses the ball. Without defensive balance and the ability to react to changes in ball possession, a team will experience trouble. These two aspects—defensive balance and the ability to react—are vitally important to all coaches, no matter how those coaches structure their transition defense.

Players use transition defense to respond to blocks, steals, rebounds, made field goals, and made free throws. Since the rebound situation is the one that teams most often encounter, transition defensive drills should be initiated with rebounding. When a ball is rebounded, the defender closest to the rebounder must either jam the rebounder or prevent him from passing the ball. This maneuver will reduce the opponent's fast-break opportunity and allow the defensive team time to react and sprint. A guard who is not back and properly balanced defensively must either stop the ball or use pressure to slow down the outlet receiver.

The player who jams the rebounder becomes the chaser. He chases the dribbler, attempting to tip or deflect the ball. The opposite front-line player sprints to the front of the rim and becomes the goal tender who prevents easy baskets.

Other players should sprint below the line of the ball, talking and matching up. They should not run to the players they are guarding. They should, instead, sprint to the middle of the court, forming a zone to take whichever player comes to them until they can switch. Once all five defenders are back, shifting to the ball side of the floor makes an opponent play five-on-five.

Following a block or a steal, a team's defensive balance and reaction awareness become severely tested. All too often, both situations place a defensive team at a disadvantage, behind the ball. Such a team should not try to stop the break high on the floor. Players should return to the lane to rebuild their defense. The more defenders there are below the line of the ball, the better.

Following a made field goal or free throw, the defense should not permit easy baskets. Reacting to a made basket automatically gives the defense time to react while the ball is inbounded. Players on the defensive team should sprint immediately, assuring that everyone is well below the line of the ball and discouraging offensive attempts to run a quick break.

Because playing transition defense is critical, transition drills should be progressive, emphasizing the most important rules.

The following symbols can be seen in the illustrations of the drills:

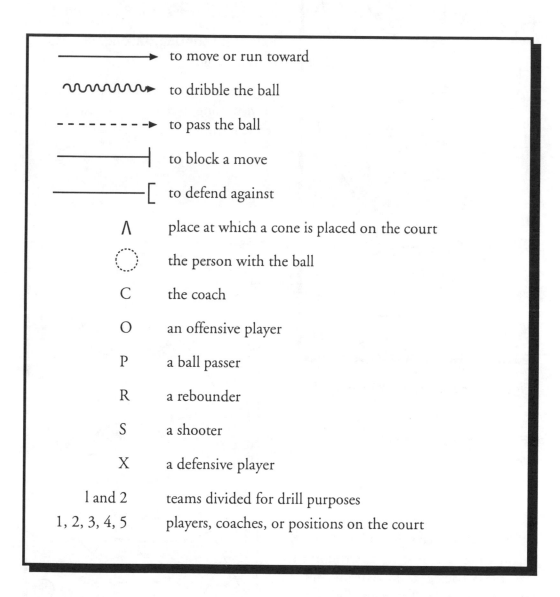

⟶	to move or run toward
∿∿∿∿∿➤	to dribble the ball
- - - - - ⟶	to pass the ball
⟞	to block a move
⟞[	to defend against
∧	place at which a cone is placed on the court
◌	the person with the ball
C	the coach
O	an offensive player
P	a ball passer
R	a rebounder
S	a shooter
X	a defensive player
1 and 2	teams divided for drill purposes
1, 2, 3, 4, 5	players, coaches, or positions on the court

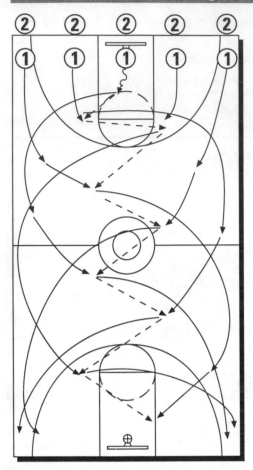

Figure 3: Five-Player Weave and React (Part 1)

Five-Player Weave and React, Part 1

Purpose: sprinting, talking, and matching up

Team 1 executes a five-player weave play, passing and going behind players while moving up the court and back.

Five-Player Weave and React, Part 2

Purpose: conditioning and communication

As team 1 lays the ball in the goal, team 2 prepares to attack by running a fast break back at team 1. Team 1 must react by sprinting below the line of the ball, talking, stopping the ball, matching up, and making team 2 attack five defenders. Team 2 uses the five lanes to maintain spacing and pressure on team 1 to half-court. Both teams play basketball once they reach half-court.

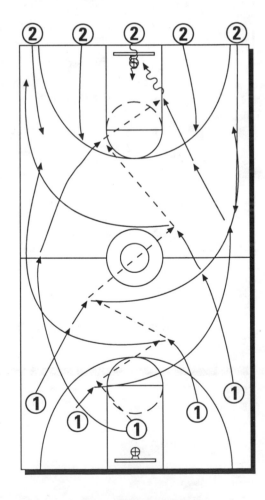

Figure 4: Five-Player Weave and React (Part 2)

Three, Two Recover

Purpose: reacting, moving below the ball, and matching up while outnumbered

This drill can be conducted a number of ways to give the offense an advantage while placing more pressure on the defense. The coach can throw the initial pass to any of the five offensive players. The offense can immediately throw the second pass.

The defensive team must sprint, talk, and match up. With offensive players having the initial advantage, this drill simulates a block or steal situation. To achieve maximum player effort, the defensive team should break back, making the offensive team execute transition defense.

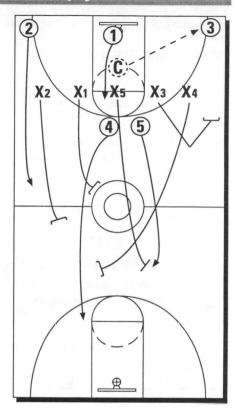

Figure 5: Three, Two Recover

Jan-and-Case Goal Tend

Purpose: having big players jam, chase, and goal tend

This drill involving four-on-four play over the full court focuses on the big players.

The coach shoots, creating a rebound. Players X4 and X5 block out and rebound or sprint to goal tend. The jammer must chase the outlet pass and try to tip the dribble. Players X1 and X2 create a passing lane or running lane, while O1 and O2 work to stop the outlet and dribble.

The offensive team must use the lanes when running the break. The defensive team has more area to cover because the drill involves four-on-four play. The defenders should break back to achieve maximum effort.

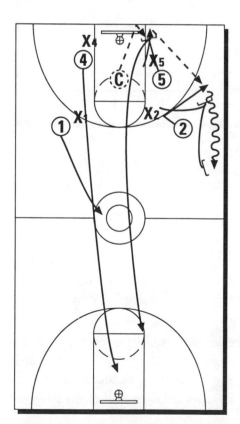

Figure 6: Jam-and-Chase Goal Tend

Five-on-Five

Purpose: practicing all transition defensive strategies

Spreading the floor in a three-out, two-in spread with some movement can place even more pressure on a defensive team. The offense cannot shoot the ball until it uses the width of the floor. The shot must then be contested.

Players X4 and X5 must block out, and X3 must block out and release from the perimeter to the board. Players X1 and X2 must prepare for the long rebound.

The offensive team must work to obtain a second shot. If the offense does get a second shot, the defensive team must run sprints. If such a shot is rebounded, the offensive team should run a fast break, and the defense must execute defensive transition rules.

This drill requires both offensive and defensive work. Again, to obtain maximum effort, players should break back.

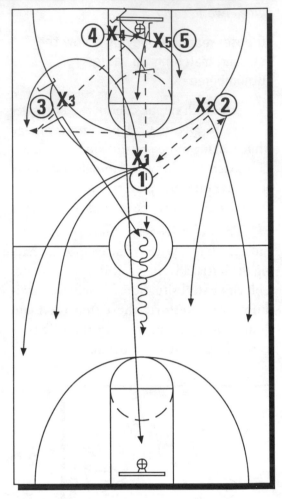

Figure 7: Five-on-Five

Within practice plans, changing the drills in a progressive manner on a daily basis will enable players to understand the rules in their entirety.

Building a defense from the 10 series (scoring area) and up the floor is mandatory. Once players execute basic rules, then a coach can be concerned about their spreading out. Not all teams are equipped to spread out defensively. Whether or not to do so is a decision the coaches and their staff must make.

The first concern all coaches have in developing a solid player-to-player defense is their players' ability to play the ball. Most players, regardless of their attitude about defense, have little knowledge of the importance of footwork. Therefore, for them to play their best defensively, coaches need to drill them daily on footwork in order to create proper habits.

One-on-One Drills

The goal of any effective defender is to keep his body between his man (the player he is guarding) and the goal. When defenders take fakes with their back foot, it creates an up-and-back movement that assures them of proper position. Theoretically, they create enough space to react to the shot, drive, or pass. Too many players take fakes, which allows them to move side to side and create all kinds of opportunities for their man. Drilling individual defensive footwork by taking fakes with their back foot creates sufficient space to drop step versus a crossover dribble, allowing the defender to control the dribble.

Rapid-Fire Footwork

Purpose: executing proper footwork; creating a habit

This simple drill remains one of the best for teaching footwork. The coach begins by using a series of foot fakes and shot fakes prior to dribbling the ball.

All five defenders in a balanced stance force the coach to dribble with his left hand and with his left foot forward. The players must take the coach's foot fakes with their back foot and move a hand up to contest his shot fakes.

As the coach dribbles the ball, the defenders must react to whatever the coach does. Players must develop their footwork to keep the other team's players in front of them and to practice contesting shots.

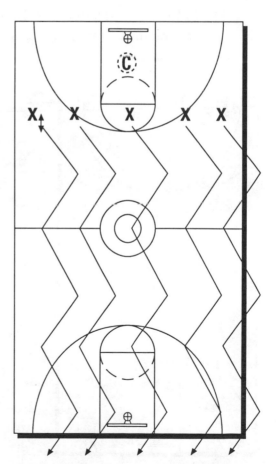

Figure 8: Rapid-Fire Footwork

Footwork and Pivots

Purpose: footwork, pivoting, and passing

Players form five lines across the baseline. The first player in each line dribbles a ball to the foul line, comes to a two-footed jump stop, and pivots back toward the baseline.

Once each player squares up to the baseline, he throws a pass to the next player in line. Each player must follow his pass and assume a defensive stance, forcing the ball handler to the left. The ball handler must throw a series of foot fakes and shot fakes to the new defensive player prior to dribbling the ball back toward the foul line. Defensive players play two dribbles before permitting the dribblers to pass and then return to the end of their lines.

The drill continues, keeping all 10 players working. This drill, although not difficult, develops essential skills.

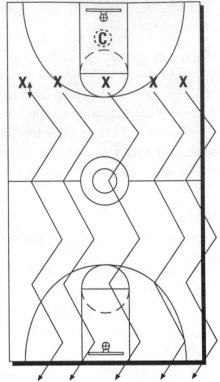

Figure 9: Footwork and Pivots

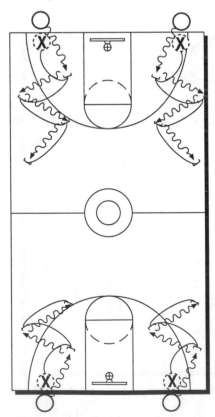

Figure 10: 10 Seconds

10 Seconds

Purpose: footwork and applying pressure to a dribbler

Players use only a quarter of the court. This setup means that the entire court can be used to keep eight players practicing at all times.

The offensive player begins out of bounds. The defensive player begins with the ball just inbounds. The defensive player hands the ball to the offensive player. Within 10 seconds, the offensive player must move the ball to half-court. Before he does, the defensive player should try to force a turnover or, at least, keep the offensive player from reaching half-court. By matching up the teams evenly and having everyone participate, the coach helps his players to develop their concentration.

Spots

Purpose: footwork, one-on-one play, and allowing no middle play

The offensive player begins one step outside of the three-point line. The defensive player, who has the ball, begins at the three-point line.

The defender gives the ball to the offensive player but tries to prevent a three-point shot. The offensive player can make a quick-decision drive or else use foot fakes to move the defender out of position while trying to reach the middle of the floor.

The defender must take all fakes with his back foot while keeping the offensive player in front and out of the middle. Defenders must also contest all shots and rebound all missed shots. Each player must defend all five spots on the floor.

Closing out on a weak side receiver may be the most difficult situation for a defender. If close outs are not drilled, a defense will more than likely break down by a simple ball-reversal play. Sprinting to within three feet of the receiver and then slowing down while assuming a defensive position will keep the defender from running beyond his player. The defender must also close out at an angle, discouraging a dribble penetration to the middle of the floor. Therefore, closing out on a weak side receiver means being able to contest a shot while staying in front, playing the dribble, and keeping the ball out of the middle of the floor. This situation is a difficult one that requires the other four defenders to be ready to help.

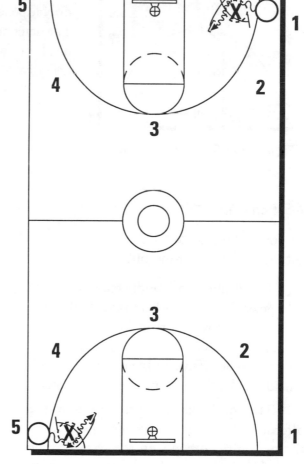

Figure 11: Spots

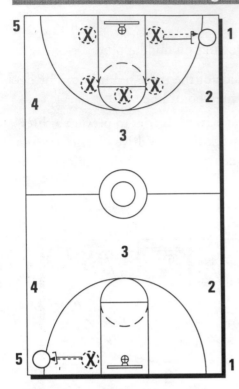

Figure 12: Spots Close Outs

Spots Close Outs

Purpose: closing out, allowing no middle play

This drill, like the spots drill, teaches players how to close out at all five spots, or places, on the floor. This drill, however, begins with a defender on the lane line passing the ball to an offensive player who is one step outside of the three-point line.

The defender must contest a three-point shot, if it is taken, and block out or play the dribble penetration to prevent a middle drive. The defender must contest all shots and then block out and rebound missed shots. Each defensive player must close out at all five spots on the floor.

React and Close Out

Purpose: reacting to a pass not anticipated and closing out

This drill can be conducted at all available goals. The coach begins with the ball while facing downcourt in front of the basket. The defender also begins by facing down the court. The offensive players begin one step outside of the three-point line on both sides.

The coach throws a pass to one of the offensive players. The defender must react to the pass and close out on the receiver. The defensive player must also contest three-point shots, take away middle drives, and retrieve the ball after rebounds. Occasionally moving the offensive players inside the three-point line can also present a challenge to the defensive players.

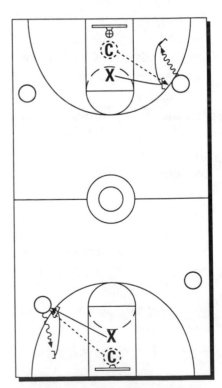

Figure 13: React and Close Out

Rotate to Close Out with Help

Purpose: creating a long rotation and close out with help

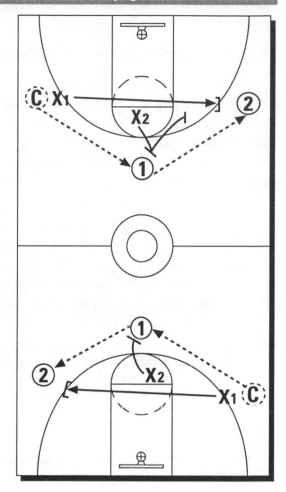

The coach has the ball while standing one step outside the three-point line on one side of the basket. Player X1 positions himself next to the coach with one hand on the coach's hip. Player O1 spots up at the top, one step outside the three-point line, while X2 plays O1 and begins moving into a helping position. Player O2 begins by standing one step outside the three-point line on the opposite side of the basket.

The coach passes the ball to O1 at the top. Player X1 sprints across the court toward O2.

Player X2 tries to slow down the pass from O1 to O2, buying time for X1. As O2 catches the ball, X1 must close out, contesting the shot if necessary, and keeping the dribble out of the middle. Player X2 drops forward to block the pass from O1 to O2. When the play becomes two-on-two, the coach steps off the court.

Figure 14: Rotate to Close Out with Help

Closing out presents difficulties for all defenders. Drilling will prove this fact to players and hopefully increase their desire to help one another. Developing team defense should be next on the agenda.

Two-on-Two

Two-on-two drills come next in the part-method approach to developing defense. Adding another defender encourages players to provide help when needed. Ball denial becomes a top priority when working two-on-two drills.

Guard-Guard Denial

Purpose: developing skills in denying and helping

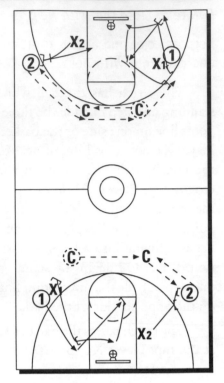

This drill requires two coaches to move the ball from guard to guard so that they shift the defenders. Player X1 must deny O1 (with the ball on his side of the court) the opportunity to catch. Player X2 must be in position to help X1 and also to prevent flash cuts by O2.

On the guard-to-guard pass, X2 must close out on O2, and X1 must move to a help position prepared so as to prevent the flash cut by O1. The ball shifts from guard to guard until a coach says, "Play." The offense then attacks and can use either coach, if necessary, but only for passing the ball. Since the coaches can only pass the ball, the drill places added pressure on the defenders.

Figure 15: Guard-Guard Denial

Three-on-Two

Purpose: close out, help, and rotate

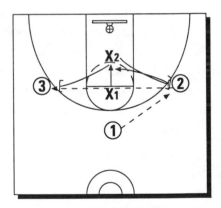

This drill begins with three offensive perimeter players moving the ball. Players X1 and X2 must work together, talking and moving, while the ball is in the air.

When the coach says, "Play," the three offensive players attack, attempting to score. Players X1 and X2 must deflect their passes, force extra passes, contest shots, and take hard fouls. If the defense gets a stop, the offense must run sprints as punishment. This drill can help develop trust among the defensive players.

Figure 16: Three-on-Two

Two-on-Two Plus One

Purpose: defending natural plays against two players plus half a player

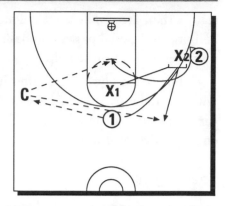

The half-player can be either a coach or an extra player who can only pass the ball to the offensive players. The offense can use the half-player at any time to apply more pressure to the two defenders. Players O1 and O2 can initiate the action any way they wish.

Figure 17: Two-on-Two Plus One

This drill should encourage the give-and-go play, as well as handoffs, isolations, pick-and-roll plays, and other random plays that can occur in games. The defensive players must work together to obtain stops.

Drilling two-on-two works well because there is little help for the individual playing the ball. With a defensive player's defeat, the offense should be able to obtain an easy basket.

Three-on-Three

Most basketball purists believe that three-on-three is the best way to teach the game. I agree, simply because of the space that can be created to give the offense an advantage. With three-on-three, offenses can now use the width of the floor, which encourages selfless play. At the same time, three-on-three places more pressure on defenders to cover more space. Three-on-three drills can be invaluable tools in developing a solid team defense.

Guar-Guard Denial with Post

Purpose: maintaining position, denial, and close outs

Two coaches, C1 and C2, fill offensive guard positions and control the drill. Players O1, O2, and O3 try to catch the ball within their areas after either C2 or C1 passes it to them. As the ball passes from guard to guard, X1, X2, and X3 must deny passes to their men by other offensive players and maintain a help position.

The three offensive players can cut to the ball, no matter where it moves, but they must

Figure 18: Guard-Guard Denial with Post

stay in their areas. The three defenders practice denying additional passes and flash cuts and remaining in position to help.

The coach says, "Play," after he is satisfied with the defensive efforts he sees. On the next catch, the offense should attack. The drill should end up three-on-three.

Screening Game

Purpose: defending various screening actions

Players O1, O2, and O3 initiate the drill with a specific screening action. The screens used to help develop proper defensive techniques should be those a team has to use to defend itself most often throughout a season.

An excellent way to conduct this drill is to make the defense guard the screen three times prior to beginning play. This gives the players a clearer understanding of the responsibilities of those who are guarding screeners and of the receivers of screens.

On the defensive guard's third attempt to defend the screen, the ball should be put in play. From this point on, the drill is run three-on-three.

Figure 19: Screening Game

Spread Game

Purpose: defending the width of the floor while maintaining one's position

Players O1, O2, and O3 should begin by spreading out on the court. They should then work to free themselves from their defenders.

After the initial pass by O1, there are few rules for the offense. The offensive players can screen away, straight cut, or use a dribble handoff while working to maintain space. At any time, back cutting to relieve pressure remains important. Giving the offense a specific number of passes it must complete prior to shooting can

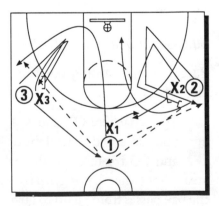

Figure 20: Spread Game

help to create offensive pressure. If the offense can produce a lay-in, however, the number of passes does not matter.

Players X1, X2, and X3 must talk, helping each other at all times to do whatever becomes necessary to obtain stops. A coach should make the drill competitive by making the losers run at the end of practice.

Four-on-Three

Purpose: rotating, closing out, and developing trust

The four offensive players pass the ball while remaining in their positions. Players X1, X2, and X3 move with each pass to cover the ball, trying to protect positions at the middle of the floor and the baseline.

Figure 21: Four-on-Three

The defender closing out on the ball must be in position to keep the ball out of the middle of the floor. The other two defenders must prepare to help the player or to help a helper.

When satisfied with his players' efforts, the coach says, "Play." The four offensive players then attack, and the three defenders must work to obtain a stop.

Hockey

Purpose: three-on-three full-court

Two rules are specific to this hockey drill: (1) the inbounds pass must be caught below the foul line, and (2) no player can cross half-court until a player dribbles the ball over the half-court line. All of the other usual rules apply.

Players X1, X2, and X3 can use any alignment to defend the inbounds pass that must be caught below the foul line. The defenders can double-team, run and jump, or play straight up while trying to steal the ball or force the offense to violate the 10-second rule.

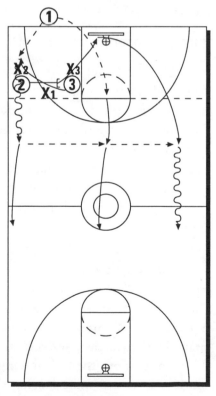

Figure 22: Hockey

Once the offense clears half-court, they should play three-on-three. At this point, the coach can determine how the offense must initiate play, or he can simply choose to allow them to play basketball. The rules remain constant, whether or not the offense scores. If the defense obtains a stop, the only rule enforced is that the ball must be dribbled across the half-court line.

Dividing an entire team into two teams, and then substituting when necessary while playing for 12–15 minutes, enhances the impact of the hockey drill. Losers should run sprints after the drill.

Four-on-Four

Adding another defender enables the defense to reduce the space on the floor. Four-on-four creates opportunities to protect the back side of a defense while covering the width of the floor much more easily. These drills should make offensive success much more difficult.

Four-on-four drills help develop a coach's basic philosophy, but they also create enough activity to work effectively against all screening actions a team encounters. Because they work well against specific screening action, four-on-four drills are very beneficial.

Five-on-Four

Purpose: covering an extra player

This drill begins at three-quarter court, which means that even more pressure will be applied on the four defenders. The five offensive players begin in a high two-one-two set. The four defenders match up, leaving their farthest receiver open, and follow this form of rotation throughout. Because of the extra receiver, it becomes essential to create ball pressure and maintain proper position.

Two guards on the offensive team bring the ball across half-court, while the three other offensive players remain in their places. The five offensive players then remain in their areas after the initial pass. They must move the ball, forcing the defenders to rotate while leaving their farthest receiver open.

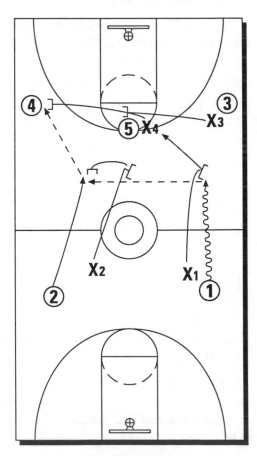

Figure 23: Five-on-Four

When the coach becomes satisfied with his players' quality of effort, he says, "Play." At that point, the offense should attack.

Four-on-Four-on-Four

Purpose: pressing, 40 series, and 10 series

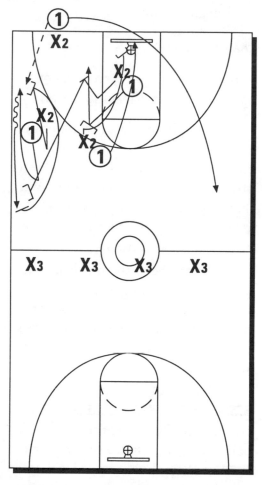

This drill effectively covers many fundamental defensive principles. Score should be kept during this drill, and the losers should run sprints.

The coach divides the team into three four-player teams—one offensive team whose players are designated as O1, and two defensive teams whose players are designated as X2 and X3. The drill begins with offensive team 1 inbounding the ball and defensive team 2 defending. Team 3 waits at half-court.

Team 1 must inbound the ball and move it over the half-court line. The players should act as if they are going to try to make a basket on the other side of the court—the opponent's side.

Defensive team 2 can apply any type of defense it chooses or whatever defense the coach wishes to employ. Defensive team 2 works to steal the ball and score or to force Team 1 to violate the 10-second rule.

Figure 24: Four-on-Four-on-Four

If team 1 moves the ball past half-court, team 2 should drop off, and team 3 should begin playing team 1. At this point, the offensive strategy that team 1 uses can be dictated by the coach, or team 1 can just play.

Team 3 should try to obtain a stop and break back at team 2 or else move the ball inbound following a score, attacking team 1 to half-court and team 2 in the front court. Team 1 should then drop off the court, while team 2 returns to play team 3.

This drill should continue until one of the teams scores a certain number of points or the time expires and the coach declares the victor.

Shell drills to help a team defend against the screening action that it will encounter throughout a season are best conducted in four-on-four situations. Obviously, there will be one less defender, which places more pressure on the four defenders to be successful. Coaches should be creative in developing their own four-on-four shell drills.

Shell Screening Action

Purpose: technique used to defend against specific screening action

This drill involves the use of the cross screen. All screening action, however, should be shelled (i.e., break down offensive play into action among fewer than five players). This move can help assure that players understand exactly how to cover all screens.

The drill begins beyond half-court with players working on ball pressure. When O1, the dribbler, arrives at the free-throw line extended, O2 cross screens for O4. Next, O4 moves around the screen toward the ball.

Players X4 and X2 provide the proper coverage to defend against the cross screen. Player O1 then passes the ball to O3, who dribbles to the opposite free-throw line extended.

Player O2 cross screens a second time for O4. Players X4 and X2 must again defend the screen.

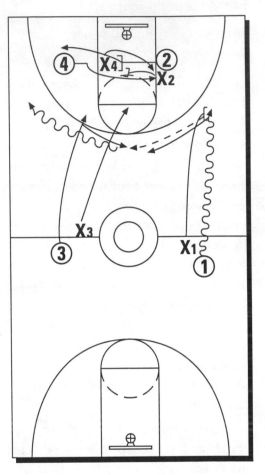

Figure 25: Shell Screening Action

Player O3 then passes the ball back to O1, and they repeat the cross screen a third time. Following this maneuver, the offense should attack by giving the ball to O4 and proceeding to play.

Five-on-Five

With five-on-five, the space on the floor becomes crowded, which forces the offensive players to maintain proper spacing in order to obtain high-quality shots. Adding a fifth defender gives the defense an advantage in that it can cover more space. More often than not, this drill involves two- or three-player games being executed against five defenders.

When the defense remains in its proper position, it has opportunities to succeed. In basketball, a game of positioning, whoever gains an advantageous position on his opponent achieves a higher rate of success than if he fails to do so.

10 Shell

Purpose: basic rules of position, rotations, and ball pressure

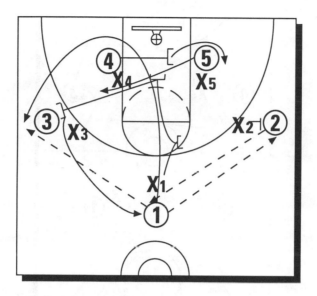

Figure 26: 10 Shell

This drill is known as the 10 shell because it works well on all of the rules for the 10 series defense. In this drill, the offensive team begins in a three-out, two-in alignment in which there are three perimeter players and two post players. Their job initially involves passing the ball from side to side to their post players, O4 and O5.

The perimeter players, O1, O2, and O3, pass the ball and exchange positions. The post players, O4 and O5, work opposite each other, using the low-post area. The defense constantly maintains its position, moving when the ball is in the air.

The emphasis remains on the defensive players' ability to create ball pressure and force the ball out of the middle, denying passes to the low post, denying the next perimeter pass, and maintaining help positions.

Once he is satisfied with his players' efforts, the coach says, "Play," and the offense attacks. The drill ends at the other end of the floor, following transition.

Five-on-Six

Purpose: creating a disadvantage

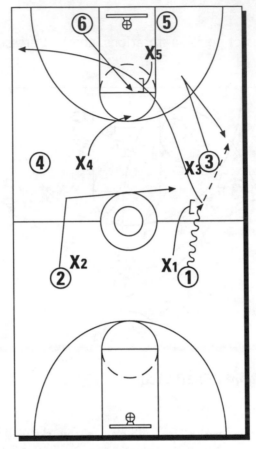

Figure 27: Five-on-Six

This drill begins with action, because the offense will work to score immediately. The offense begins in a two, two, and two alignment at three-quarter court with ball pressure.

Players O3 and O4 must free themselves without any screens. From the point of the initial pass, O1, O2, O3, and O4 must either goal cut or exchange positions with one another.

The two post players, O5 and O6, play off of one another, using the entire key area. The six offensive players need to be aggressive and well spaced and constantly look for opportunities for lay-ins or open jump shots.

The defense must counter the offense's aggression. Defending six offensive players with constant movement places enormous pressure on the defense's ability to obtain stops. This drill can develop high levels of trust and, ultimately, confidence among the defensive players.

Cutthroat

Purpose: succeeding with defense first

This drill emphasizes the value of defense, as well as the value of moving forward offensively as the result of defense. In order to score a point in this game, a team must make a stop defensively and then score at the other end. This drill emphasizes the proper balance that a good-quality team must have in its performance.

Three teams play. Team 1 begins on defense. Team 2 begins on offense. Team 3 prepares to step on the court to play offense.

The drill begins at three-quarter court with ball pressure. Team 2, the offense, works to score in order to obtain the chance to play defense.

If team 2 (offense) scores, team 1 (defense) leaves the court. Team 2 then becomes the defense, and team 3 becomes the offense.

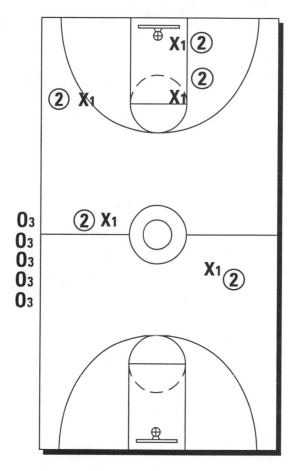

Figure 28: Cutthroat

If team 1 (defense) gets a stop and scores at the other end, however, it stays on as defense, while team 3 becomes the offense. If team 1 (defense) gets a stop but fails to score at the other end, team 2 (offense) becomes the defense, and team 3 becomes the offense. In order to score, a team must get a stop and a basket.

Again, conducting shell drills to defend against certain frequently used screening action becomes time well spent in the overall development of the team's defense.

Chapter 4

A Philosophy of Offense

Offensive Strategies

Offense helps a team win. Offense fuels a defense.

The best teams understand the value of points produced directly from their effective defensive work. They know that supplementing their offense with easy baskets from their defense leads to achieving the differential needed to reach their goals. In the process, they achieve a balanced performance that makes them more difficult to defeat.

Offensive pressure with a premium on easy baskets has long been my offensive philosophy. All coaches should work to help players reduce their opponent's ability to make easy baskets or increase their team's ability to make easy baskets.

Offensive pressure should be a constant within a team's performance. Such pressure promotes using the length and width of the floor, using maximum space that the defense must cover. A team initiates pressure by reacting to blocks, steals, rebounds, made field goals, made free throws, and a shifting defense produced by the purpose and organization of an offense. Offensive pressure executed with purpose, timing, courage, and efficiency can produce easy basket opportunities and also fuel a defense. Offense should be played this way as often as possible throughout a game.

Producing easy baskets takes selfless, aggressive play in three areas of the game: transition, offensive rebounding, and free throws.

Transition

Transition that is executed with a purpose and that uses the entire court puts the ultimate pressure on five defenders because of the space they must cover. Transition offense is created by literally everything that occurs as a result of defensive efforts. The most important aspect in offensive transition is reacting to the possession of the ball and sprinting with space while looking for the ball. In the process of reacting and sprinting with space and purpose, a team applies pressure with a sense of organization.

Developing offensive transition also takes a commitment by players simply because of the hard work and discipline involved. A team's best hope is to have a point guard who is capable of throwing the ball ahead to runners. If runners do not catch often enough, they will not sprint with as great a sense of urgency. As a result, offensive pressure may diminish. The other major goal remains teaching point guards when transition opportunities are available and when they are not—when they should force the break or back off.

The offensive pressure produced in transition must be executed with a definite purpose at the proper times. There is never an advantage when players are out of control. Players must play in balance within the confines of a plan. Transition offense must be executed as a team.

Offensive Rebounding

Players must also learn that offensive rebounding allows them to produce easy baskets. With the addition of the three-point shot, teams that emphasize offensive rebounding began obtaining more shots and easy baskets. The missed three-point shot rebounds higher and longer, giving the players more space to cover. As a result, there is more pressure placed on defensive rebounding, forcing players to block out better, creating floor space to obtain an angle on the ball to increase air space. The long rebounds are left for the guards to react to and run down. Players must learn that the missed three-point shot creates more opportunities for offensive rebounding.

When teams work to force a contested shot, only to give up an offensive rebound and two points, they can feel devastated. When teams give up an offensive rebound on a missed free throw, it becomes ridiculous. When the flow of a transition defense is late and the overachieving opponent tips in a contested missed layup, it becomes intolerable. Offensive rebounding is the only aspect of the game in which selfishness benefits the team's performance. If players are willing to force their will on the offensive board because they want to score, the team will benefit, as long as the players do not take poor shots.

The ability to create offensive rebounding opportunities results from dribble penetration. Such opportunities occur because of the spacing that an offense creates, along with the players' ability to read the defense and make quick decisions. When the decision is made to penetrate, they must use two dribbles in order to make a difference.

Many times, the second dribble clears the way for the third dribble, forcing the opponent's big players to help and open up the offensive board. When big players are forced to help defend against dribble penetration, they are then in position for scoring passes and offensive rebounds. They must, however, learn how to create the proper angles in order to be successful. For all of these reasons, making offensive rebounding a priority makes sense.

Free Throws

A third area of basketball that produces easy points is the free throw. Players who reach the foul line are courageous, tough-minded physical types. All players, however, must realize that reaching the foul line to shoot free throws can make the difference between winning and losing.

Although the rules of the game favor the offense, this factor only makes a difference when a team takes advantage of the rules. Players must know when to move and to create straight angles to the basket. Players must also develop an aggressive attitude regarding creating contact. They make a mistake by searching for contact or initiating contact.

Taking advantage of the rules means creating contact through straight angles to the basket. These opportunities are realized when players make quick, aggressive decisions or force their defender to move out of position through well-executed ball, head, or foot fakes.

Offensive pressure is created all over the floor and can produce easy baskets that fuel an offense. At the same time, while manufacturing offensive rebounds and free-throw opportunities, a team keeps its opponent out of the open court a high percentage of the time, making the players attack all five of their defenders. Throughout the course of the game, this strategy can pay dividends and improve a team's defensive effort. This strategy is another example of creating a proper balance within a team's performance.

Offensive Organization

Coaches should communicate their offensive philosophy to their players. They first need to explain how the offensive court can be analyzed. Players, again, will retain more of what they see than what they hear. Since creating space within all of an offense is essential, organizing the court becomes essential.

Understanding the Court's Organization

Along with the concepts of offensive pressure and transition, spacing must be understood and consistently executed. I divide the offensive court into five running lanes—two outside lanes, two inside lanes, and the middle lane. Ideally, the outside running lanes are for the 2 and 3 players. The inside lanes are for the 4 and 5 players (the center and the big forward). The middle lane is for the point guard. (See Figure 29.)

At times, however, the 4's, the 5's, and the point guard will use different lanes. Creating these five running lanes can facilitate a transition defense. The fast break, early offense, quicks, and press offense will be spaced better by using this technique.

While teaching the half-court offense, a coach may find that running-lane lines and a three-point line can help players visualize the space needed for them to be successful. If possible, marking these lanes on a court with either erasable paint or tape throughout the preseason can be extremely helpful in developing proper running and spacing habits.

Determining the Average Number of Shots to Take per Game

Once players understand the court's organization, they need to determine how many shots to average per game. The number is dependent on the length of the games.

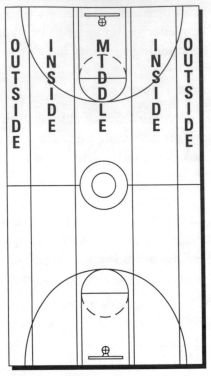

Figure 29: The offensive court

The best teams in the NBA want 85–90 shots a game. One must determine how many of these shots will be produced by transition, set plays, plays after time-outs, and out-of-bounds plays.

When a team becomes committed to running in all possible situations, 45–50 percent of its shots will be produced in transition. Thus, about 40 percent of the remaining shots must be produced by set plays or quarter-court offense. The remaining 10–15 percent of the shots will be produced by out-of-bounds plays and plays after time-outs or at the beginning of halves or quarters.

Establishing a benchmark for shots produced according to one's philosophy of offensive pressure will determine the game goals. Players will then become accustomed to this process, which is vital to the success of a team.

Transition Techniques

The transition portion of an offense consists of four parts: press alignment, fast break, early offense, and quicks. All four should be executed from the same organization to create simplicity.

Press Alignment

Press alignment should be the first concern. When teams spread out defensively, the goal is to make them pay by attacking them in an organized fashion, looking for a layup or high-percentage shot by the proper player, with the board covered for second-shot opportunities. The only time a team does not attack a full-court press is in late-game situations. Press alignment will probably be used the least by a team protecting a lead. The strategy, however, is just as important as all other parts of a transition offense—and sometimes more important.

Losing a game in the final two minutes because a team cannot defeat the press can be devastating. Coaches should constantly work on their team's press alignment.

The Fast Break

The fast-break portion of transition offense results directly from effective defensive work. These fast-break points can make an enormous difference in a game.

A good-quality fast break is the result of proper reaction to the possession of the ball. Reacting quickly, sprinting with space, and playing in a selfless manner are essential in earning layups or making high-percentage shots with the board covered. Fast breaks are created by blocks, steals, and rebounds. Each situation can place the defense in a different position.

The true fast-breaking team, however, will sprint in all situations in order to obtain those all-important second shots. Teams committed to offensive pressure sometimes must run to be running. This strategy can pay dividends.

The initial thrust of a break is essential. When an opponent takes away a first option, however, a break ending must produce ball reversal, placing added pressure on an opponent's transition defense. Using the width of the floor can consistently open up scoring opportunities. The key is maintaining pressure offensively. To pull the ball out to run a set play attacking five set defenders can eliminate any advantage a break creates.

Early Offense

The early offense within a transition philosophy creates pressure that defines running teams. Early offense is run only after made field goals. Like the fast break, effective early offense is born from reaction. In this case, the team reacts to a made field goal.

Bringing the ball inbounds to the point guard must be done quickly and efficiently. The running lanes must be filled with the proper players, assuring adequate spacing.

From this point, looking for the easy basket becomes the main priority. The point guard must move the ball ahead to the runners whenever possible, or they will not run as they should. (I've never seen a player outrun or outdribble a pass.)

Defining the nature of an excellent shot can help assure an efficient, organized early offense. Most teams can obtain contested jump shots at any time.

When an opponent takes away the early basket option, a team's organization must produce the reversal pass. Once again, shifting the defense can provide an effective offense.

Quicks

Quicks are quick-hitting plays run out of transition after made free throws. This separate group of plays can help players take advantage of mismatches, exploit offensive strengths, and produce quick shots and three-point shots when necessary. Most of the time, quicks are one- or two-option plays. The team benefits because players maintain pressure and give the opponent a different play to defend.

When working the clock at the end of a quarter or a half, players must learn the value of quicks to the two-shots-for-one concept. Quicks can also help players catch up in scoring and even move ahead. Over the years, the quick series has come in handy.

With the quick series, unlike the fast break and early offense, players need to be given calls. I use numbers to keep calls simple. The number usually identifies the two positions highlighted in the play. For example, quick 24 is a back-pick set by the 2 guard for the big forward 4 player. However quicks are labeled, they should be simple to remember.

The Quarter-Court Offense

The quarter-court offense is the next concern. This portion of an offense will produce approximately 40 percent of a team's shots. Therefore, whatever a coach decides to run, it must fit the team and be taught properly.

The passing game remains popular for a variety of reasons. The game produces movement, requires players to read defenses, uses the width of the floor, and involves all the players.

Flex is a popular structured style of passing game. Continuity offenses help maintain structured movement to some degree and, at the same time, use the entire width of the floor highlighted with triangles. Set plays with two or three options can be highly successful, because everyone is placed in a position of strength.

Every style of quarter-court offense has its strengths and weaknesses. The coach should therefore work to eliminate the weaknesses. He can accomplish this goal by stressing to his players the importance of the following concepts:

- Maintaining triangles can help the players see all their receivers and also help them to handle double-teaming.
- Rebounders must maintain the proper position as they prepare to rebound.
- A team's organization must facilitate play at both ends of the court.
- Spacing must be maintained at 10–12 feet.

- The offense must penetrate the defense.
- Player strengths should be highlighted.

A coach's offensive philosophy in the quarter-court must also provide for enough depth to handle the adversity every season presents. If shooters do not always make their shots, the offense should try to produce high-percentage shots for those shooters to help them gain confidence. If a team is sluggish, an offense must create movement to produce more aggressiveness. If the best offensive player suffers injuries or does not earn the academic grades needed to play, a coach must move in another direction to highlight the strengths of other players in order to succeed.

A quarter-court offense must include an offense highlighting five-player movement to create aggressiveness and activity as needed. Shooters can use baseline screens or back-pick plays. Inside players can use post-up plays. Isolation plays can help dribble-drive players. Point guards can use pick-and-roll plays. These can be separate plays, or they can be part of a passing game or a continuity offense.

A coach must simply cover all bases in case of adversity. The benefit of creating opportunities for players with different strengths can be surprising. Coaches can end up developing weapons of which they were previously unaware.

Special Plays

Developing a special group of plays or options out of a basic offense for post–time-out situations can produce easy baskets or, at least, high-percentage shots. Post–time-out plays and out-of-bounds plays can produce approximately 10 percent of a team's shots. This part of an offense may seem minor, but all of the minor aspects add up. The same attention should be given to all aspects of an offense.

Out-of-bounds plays naturally create an advantage for the defense, simply because they are all four versus five. For this reason, the player who takes the ball out of bounds must be an effective passer, maintain his composure, and be a threat after the pass so that he forces five-on-five coverage. Some out-of-bounds plays will produce effective shots when the weak side of the play is the first option and the strong side produces the second or third option.

Moving a set defense is a must. For the most part, baseline out-of-bounds plays are similar. Being so close to the basket, however, they create more opportunities for the inbound passer to produce points. This becomes an excellent way for coaches to give less-skilled players the opportunity for shots that will help them feel more a part of the offense.

Offensive Goals

The creation and organization of an offensive philosophy by the coach yields the goals necessary to achieve success. Both establishing goals and being aware of players' success rates in achieving them remain essential.

An assistant coach can be responsible for charting a team's offense. Such an individual can then give a head coach an accurate assessment of what is going well and what needs work. This process can help a head coach make proper adjustments or change his play calls. Ultimately, the coaching staff can always do a more efficient job of helping the team reach its offensive goals.

Assist-to-Turnover Ratio

The goal that most affects an offense is one related to the assist-to-turnover ratio. Because of the style of play and offensive pressure inherent in the game, and because basketball is a team game, efficient ball movement is essential. In the NBA, coaches want a minimum of 25 assists and a maximum of 15 turnovers per game. These numbers can produce a 2:1 ratio in most games. This goal should help a team reach a field-goal–attempt mark of 85–90 shots per game.

Rebounding the Offensive Board

The goal that next affects success the most is that which is related to success in rebounding the offensive board. As discussed earlier, rebounding is a major part of offensive pressure. Helping players see the significance of this goal is imperative.

In the NBA, coaches want a minimum of 15 rebounds per game. The number of offensive rebounds available is directly related to a team's field-goal percentage. Therefore, the number will vary. Establishing a goal that might be difficult to reach, however, is essential.

Reaching the Foul Line and Making Free Throws

Reaching the foul line and making free throws is a third part of offensive pressure. Obtaining this goal can further affect a player's mind-set and help the offense. In the NBA, coaches want a team to attempt 30 free throws per game and make 75 percent of them. Both of these goals are difficult for a team to achieve. Offensive goals must be lofty, but reachable.

Field-Goal Percentage

The final major offensive goal is adequate field-goal percentage. The chances of achieving a high percentage of shots can be increased by improving the assist-to-turnover ratio and working on the offensive board. In the NBA, coaches want players to hit 48–50 percent of their shots from the floor. Again, shooting this well as a team is not simple, but it is possible if easy baskets become a priority.

The specific goals set for an offense depend on the style of play and length of the game. The goals set by NBA coaches are based on 48-minute games with a 24-second shot clock. Therefore, goals set for 32-minute games or 40-minute games will obviously be lower.

Establishing difficult but reachable offensive goals helps to promote an aggressive style of play. The aggressor usually succeeds.

Offensive Drills

Achieving offensive pressure requires the use of drills designed to develop offensive skills. Players should engage in such drills in preseason and pre-practice sessions, as well as during the off-season. Practice time should be reserved for team development.

Conditioning always remains necessary in basketball. To maintain pressure offensively and defensively, a team must be in excellent physical condition.

Drills that reflect a coach's style of play should occur during every practice. Passing and catching are two fundamental skills that should be developed.

Conducting the same drills daily can ensure conditioning, confidence, and levels of mental toughness. Ultimately, a team should execute its running drills with flawless precision.

Pre-Practice Drills

Pre-practice sessions usually allow for 30 minutes of work. These sessions should be planned so that the coaching staff can teach and reinforce all the drills.

Creating stations and then rotating the players from station to station can help ensure that all the players do the proper work. The following six drills can be used during such sessions.

Pivot to Pass

Purpose: pivoting, balance, and passing

Each player lines up on the baseline with a partner. The first player dribbles to the foul line, comes to a jump stop, and executes an outside pivot or inside pivot while properly balanced. Following the pivot, the player throws a chest pass or bounce pass back to his partner and returns to the line.

When the coach becomes satisfied with the quality of effort, each player dribbles to the foul line, uses a change-of-direction dribble, and continues down the court using

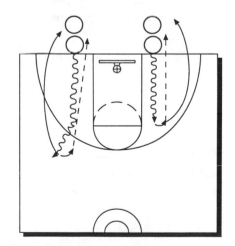

Figure 30: Pivot to Pass

three more dribbles before coming to a jump stop and pivoting. Finally, the dribbler uses a baseball pass to return the ball to his partner.

Half-Court Fast Break

Purpose: pivoting, dribbling, passing, and post move

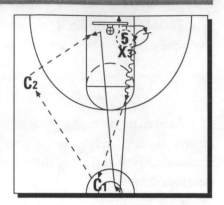

This drill can help condition front-line players to react to jammed rebounds and initiate fast breaks. The drill should be conducted on both sides of the free-throw lane and the middle.

Player O5 begins with the ball on the right side facing the court. A defender begins right behind player O5. One coach stands at half-court, and another stands on the opposite wing.

Figure 31: Half-Court Fast Break

Player O5 throws the ball off the backboard, producing a rebound. Next, O5 pivots to the outside, looking to outlet the ball. The defender, however, jams the rebounder, forcing him to step through and pivot to the middle of the floor. Following the pivot, player O5 must use three dribbles to clear the jammer and then pass the ball to the coach at half-court.

The rebounder continues to run to half-court to touch the line, pivot, and sprint to either the opposite low-post area or the front of the rim. At that point, he receives a pass from the coach on the wing and executes a post move. The player who jammed the rebounder should also meet the offensive player on the opposite block to defend the post move.

Two-Player Game Shooting

Purpose: feeding the post, making game shots

Player O1 begins beyond half-court with X1 prepared to defend. Player O5 begins on the right or left block with X5 prepared to defend. A coach with a ball begins on the opposite elbow.

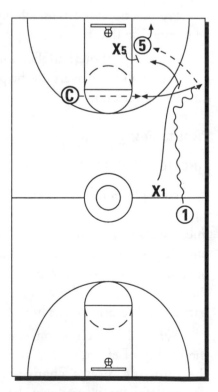

Player O1 dribbles the ball to the free-throw line extended (elbow). Player X1 defends and tries to make it difficult for O1 to feed the ball to O5. Player O5 receives the ball from O1 and tries to score while defending against X5.

Figure 32: Two-Player Game Shooting

Following the pass, player O1 must then slide toward the baseline or the top of the circle. The coach passes the ball to O1, who prepares to shoot. Player X1 must work to contest O1's shot.

Offensive Rebounding

Purpose: offensive rebounding, footwork shooting

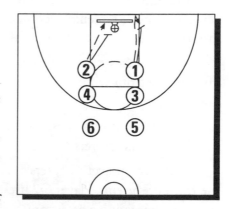

Front-line players form two lines inside the elbow areas. Each player should have a basket-ball. The players alternate so as to reduce the possibility of injury. Each player will take five shots, one at a time.

The first player, O1, throws the ball off the backboard, simulating a rebound. On this first shot, the player should rebound the ball in the air and lay the ball over the rim.

Figure 33: Offensive Rebounding

Player O2 then follows after O1 makes his shot. Player O3 follows O2, and so on.

The second time through the drill, the players must rebound the ball in the air and also make and name their shot by using the backboard. The third time through, they must rebound the ball in the air, but land in a balanced position, ball fake, and power the ball to the basket using the backboard. The fourth time through, they must again land in a balanced position and ball fake. They must, however, pivot away without using a dribble and then shoot a jump hook shot. The fifth time through, they must rebound the ball in the air and dunk the ball if possible. If they cannot dunk it, they must repeat one of the other shots.

The players change lines after everyone has executed the five shots. Changing lines assures that all the players will develop skill with their weak hand.

Pass and Catch

Purpose: passing

This drill has been used for years. It is still effective in pre-practice sessions.

Players facing one another form two lines approximately 15 feet apart. They then work on the following: two-handed chest passes, two-handed bounce passes, pivoting following a ball fake, and passes thrown behind their back.

Two-Ball Shooting

Purpose: footwork and shooting

Breaking down an offense into shooting drills can be time well spent. Having players simulate screening action and giving both players shots not only helps their shooting skills, but also their total understanding of the offense.

Two coaches or a single coach and a manager can conduct this drill. Players must know from whom they are receiving passes. The example shown is of a pin-down action.

Players form two lines, one on the baseline and one on the wing. The coaches pass balls to the players in line.

The wing player, O1, sets a screen for O2, who sets his man up by moving to the front of the rim. Player O2 uses O1's screen, preparing to shoot the elbow jump shot after receiving a pass from coach 1.

Player O1 pivots or slips to the rim as O2 uses his screen. Coach 2 passes the ball to O1. All players must retrieve their ball and return it to the coach who passed it to them.

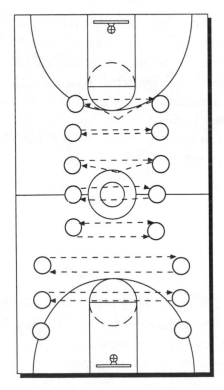

Figure 34: Pass and Catch

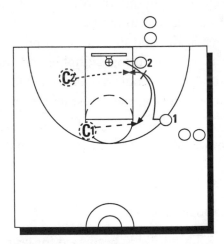

Figure 35: Two-Ball Shooting

Three Out

Purpose: warm-up period, running, and passing

With players forming three lines along the baseline, the players in front begin running a three-player weave down the court, using five passes. When each group reaches the foul line, the next group takes off.

After two trips per line, or on the coach's command, each group runs a three-player weave using four passes.

The coach says, "Three passes," once he is satisfied with the quality of his players' efforts. The players continue to run a three-player weave using only three passes. The fewer the passes, the harder they run. Five minutes of this drill should provide the players with ample warm-up.

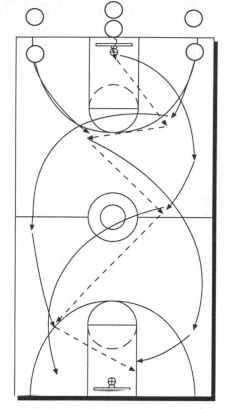

Figure 36: Three Out

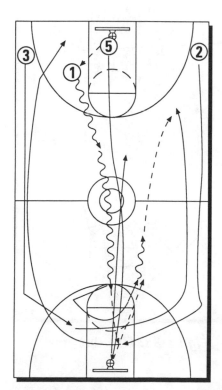

Figure 37: Four Out

Four Out

Purpose: running with proper space, ballhandling, and conditioning

Four players fill four lanes of the possible five lanes on the offensive court (refer to Figure 29). Runners line up in the outside lanes. The point guards line up in the middle lane, while the front-line players (4 and 5, forwards and centers) line up in the inside lane.

To begin the drill, a front-line player throws a ball off the board, simulating a rebound, and then rebounds the ball and outlets to the point guard.

The runners react by remaining in their lanes while running as the ball is rebounded. The point guard pushes the ball with a dribble or two and throws the ball ahead to one of the runners.

The receiver then lays the ball in the basket and sprints to the opposite outside lane. The runner who does not catch a ball must circle at the broken line and sprint to the opposite outside lane.

The front-line player trails his teammates on the fast break and must retrieve the ball from the net. That player then throws the ball to the point guard, who circles back up the court throwing the ball to the runner ahead, who lays the ball in the basket. The trailer must move beyond half-court as the ball goes through the net.

The next four players react to the layup and the sprint by running the same drill. They do not start over again. Instead, the next trailer simply takes the ball out of the net and the next group begins.

After running four out, the team plays four out twice. The coach conducts the drill in the same way, except that the players go up and down twice. On the final trip, the trailer must sprint the length of the floor and lay the ball in. Running four out twice helps to condition the players effectively and also forces big players to run the floor.

Five Out

Purpose: conditioning, spacing, and break work

Five players fill all five lanes. A coach conducts the drill like the four-out drill, except that there are two trailers instead of one.

Player O5, the first trailer, retrieves the ball from the net and passes it to O4, the second trailer. Player O4 then passes the ball to O1, the point guard, who must release it farther up the court. Players should run five out twice and without the ball hitting the floor.

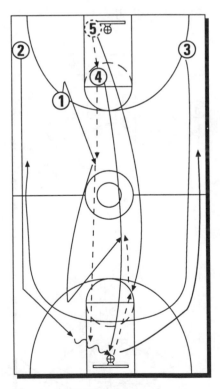

Figure 38: Five Out

Continuing to run remains important for players. Obtaining mental exercise regarding set plays and transition, however, can be achieved in the make-miss drill. Properly spacing the offense and working on timing both become necessary for successful execution. Running this drill daily can show players how to execute an entire offensive strategy.

Make-Miss

Purpose: practice set plays to transition offense without a defense

This drill helps teams that use different endings to fast breaks and early offenses. The drill provides a team with the opportunity to differentiate between the two strategies.

The offensive players run a set play, but can take only one shot. If they make the shot, they take the ball out of bounds and simulate the early offense to the other end of the floor. If they miss the shot, they react by running the fast break back.

Once a team scores, the next team prepares to step on the court to run a set play and then react by either making the shot or missing it and running. This drill allows a team to practice simulating an entire offense and also enhances the players' conditioning.

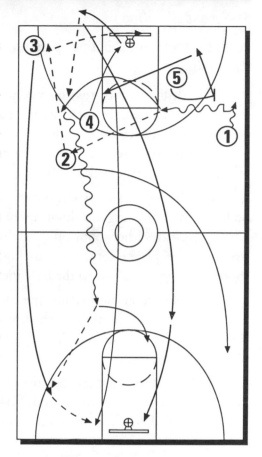

Figure 39: Make-Miss

Shooting Drills

A team's ability to shoot always affects its success. Practicing proper shooting form and obtaining game shots must become part of practice drills.

The offense should be divided into shooting drills to ensure that players take the shots that they will take during games. They will benefit by becoming familiar with spots on the floor where the offense will likely produce shots during live action.

The 55-second shooting drill (Figure 40) can give players high-quality shots all around the perimeter. The three-player rotate drill (Figure 41) can ensure that they get valuable perimeter shots with pressure. The perimeter follow-the-leader drill enables players to obtain a variety of shots from their particular areas of the court. The follow-the-leader post drill gives front-line players footwork shooting opportunities in all essential areas.

55-Second Shooting

Purpose: footwork shooting, passing, and rebounding

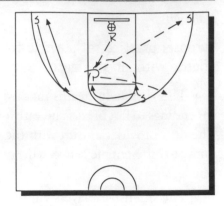

This drill works best with three players and two basketballs. The shooter (S) begins on the baseline. The passer begins on the opposite elbow from the shooter. The rebounder begins in front of the basket.

The shooter begins by cutting to the elbow and then catching and shooting the ball. The player can either shoot off a catch or a dribble. The player continues cutting and shooting from the elbow to the baseline for 55 seconds.

Figure 40: 55-Second Shooting

The rebounder must return the ball to the passer as quickly as possible, keeping his arms up in the air as each shot is in the air, and move to the ball prior to rebounding. The passer must make perfect passes to the shooter using either a chest pass or a bounce pass.

Players rotate into these positions until all three have shot from the two spots. Next, they move to the elbows and, finally, to the opposite wing and baseline. The organization of this drill allows a coach to teach his players the proper shooting footwork.

Three-Player Rotate

Purpose: footwork shooting against a defense

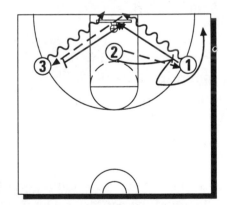

This drill involves three players and one basketball. The players should take shots within their range.

Player O1 begins under the basket with the ball. Players O2 and O3 begin spotted up, prepared to shoot. Player O1 passes to O2 and follows the pass, contesting O2's shot.

Figure 41: Three-Player Rotate

Following the shot, player O2 then retrieves the ball and passes it to O3, contesting O3's shot. Each shooter should move to set up his defender prior to the catch.

This drill develops players' skill in shooting off the catch or off the dribble. Requiring players to make quick-decision drives past the defender who is attempting to contest shots becomes time well spent.

Perimeter Follow the Leader

Purpose: practicing game shots

This drill primarily involves perimeter players. In it, each player with a ball follows the leader.

The drill begins at half-court with the first player speed dribbling to the right elbow and then pulling up for a jump shot. The second time through, the player shoots from the left elbow. The third time, the player speed dribbles to the right elbow and changes direction back to the left, taking a short jump shot at the broken line inside of the free-throw lane. The fourth time, the player speed dribbles left and changes direction back to the right, taking a short jump shot at the broken line. The fifth time through, the player drives hard right, changing direction back to the left and shooting a left-handed baby hook shot. The sixth time, the player must drive hard to the left elbow, change direction back to the right, and shoot a baby right-handed hook shot.

Players move from the top of the floor to the baseline. The first player passes the ball to the coach, sets up his man, and cuts to the elbow, prepared to shoot a jump shot. The second time through, the player fades to the corner for the jump shot. These shots must be taken on both sides of the floor.

Next, the players remain on the baseline and simulate a back-pick play prior to stepping to the ball and receiving a pass from the coach. Again, players must practice the back pick on both sides of the court.

Next, the players move the line to a guard position. After this, they pass the ball to the coach and use a simulated screen for a flare to the wing. Again, players must use both sides of the floor.

Coaches can develop their own follow-the-leader drills for perimeter players to help develop their shooting skills.

Follow the Leader—Post

Purpose: footwork shooting

Each post player should begin with a ball on a wing, with the coach on the opposite wing. The first player throws a two-handed bounce pass to the coach, sets up his defender, and sprints to the foul-line area.

The first time through, each player shoots a jump shot. The second time, each makes a quick-decision straight drive into a baby hook shot. The third time, each makes a quick-decision cross over into a baby hook shot on the opposite side. The fourth time, each makes a quick-decision straight drive with one dribble into a jump shot. The fifth time, each makes a quick-decision crossover with one dribble into a jump shot. The sixth time, each makes a quick-decision straight drive into a change-of-direction dribble, finishing with a baby hook shot. The seventh time, each makes a quick-decision crossover into a change-of-direction dribble, finishing with a baby hook shot.

Moving the line to the low-post area prepares players for the next part of the drill. The players again throw two-handed bounce passes to the coach. They must set up their defender and move across the lane to the low-post area.

On the catch the first time, the players square up to the baseline for a jump shot. The second time, they square up in the lane for a jump shot. The third time, they square up on the baseline and step through, shooting a baby hook shot. The fourth time, they square up in the lane and step through into a power layup. The fifth time, they use the two-dribble move, middle-shooting either a jump hook shot or a jump shot. The sixth time, they use a two-dribble move to the middle lane and drop-step back to the basket, shooting either a baby hook shot or a dunk.

Next, the players step off the low post toward the sideline approximately 15 feet. The coach moves to the elbow on the players' side of the floor. The first time, they shoot the jump shot. The second time, they make a straight quick-decision drive with one dribble to take a jump shot. The third time, they make a quick-decision crossover with one dribble to take a jump shot.

Finally, the players line up along the baseline facing the basket. The coach moves to the front side of the rim to face the players. The first player throws the ball to the coach while preparing to catch a lob pass and either dunk the ball or bring it down and power it back up.

Coaches should utilize the follow-the-leader post drill series using both sides of the court. Because of the inordinate length of time these drills take, alternating sides every other day works well. All shots should be followed so that the players can work on their offensive rebounding.

Drills to Teach Pure Basketball

It is essential that the coach set aside a block of time in practice to teach players how to play offensive basketball. Throughout any given season, numerous possessions will occur that will break down an offense; therefore, players must learn to react and play basketball.

Teams with players who have a thorough knowledge of the game will have the best chance to succeed. Most offenses involve three-player games; therefore, playing three-on-three becomes a great way to teach offensive basketball.

Effective offensive play requires players to learn the value of several strategies. These include the following: strong position (triple threat, or maintaining a proper athletic stance, with the knees bent and the body prepared to move, before shooting, passing, or dribbling the ball); spacing; screening; reading screens; receiving screens; relieving ball pressure; knowing when to move, pass, and shoot; movement; and using the width of the floor.

The only way to teach players how to play effectively on offense is to place them in situations that enable them to learn the proper techniques. Coaches should conduct drills requiring three-on-three play to emphasize the strategies listed above.

Three-on-Three

Purpose: playing basketball

The drill, which presents a great opportunity for the coach to teach basketball, begins beyond half-court with ball pressure. Starting players O2 and O3 on each wing creates the spacing needed to initiate play. These players will have to free themselves from their defenders in order to relieve ball pressure at any given time.

Once O1 passes the ball to either O2 or O3, he should read the defense and either goal cut or screen away for the opposite wing. From that point, the three offensive players should work to maintain space and movement, screen for each other, read defenders, and produce high-quality shots.

Coaches should create drills that emphasize efficient offensive play. Offensive pressure requires not only an aggressive mind-set, but also an aggressively efficient approach. Playing four-on-four with specific rules regarding the number of passes that can be made and using the width of the floor can teach players to maintain a balanced athletic stance when dealing with the ball. This scenario will also help them learn to set screens effectively and make sound decisions regarding their passes.

Figure 42 Three-on-Three

Efficient

Purpose: screening and passing

This drill works best with four offensive players who begin beyond half-court. Offensively, they must first complete five legitimate 15-foot passes.

They must then free a specific player for a specific shot. To succeed in this drill, players must set up their defenders to receive screens and set screens well. The offensive players must take care of the ball and make sound decisions.

The four defenders must work to pressure the ball, deny passes, and deflect and steal the ball.

Offensive Rebounding Drills

Effective offensive rebounding remains one of the best ways to create offensive pressure. Coaches must teach front-line players how to remain even with their defenders. Placing players in competitive drills can help them develop the proper techniques they will need in order to create second-shot opportunities.

Second Shot

Purpose: offensive rebounding

This drill works best by playing four-on-four. If possible, coaches should use a smaller rim, or else cover the rim, so they can produce more rebounding opportunities.

The team consists of three four-on-four teams. Players earn points by grabbing offensive rebounds. Thus, staying on the offensive becomes essential.

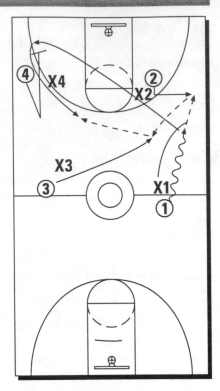

Figure 43: Efficient

Team 1 begins on offense, team 2 begins on defense, and team 3 prepares to go on defense.

The offense begins beyond half-court and must use the width of the floor prior to making a shot. The defense tries to steal the ball, deflect passes, contest shots, block out, and rebound. The offensive team tries to produce high-quality first shots, as well as second shots.

In this drill, the offense must secure the ball and set up effective second shots in order to score points. An effective tip-in counts toward the point total.

Team 3 then goes on defense and the drill continues. Requiring that the teams score seven points can help develop the players' skill in offensive rebounding. Players on the two teams that lose must run as punishment.

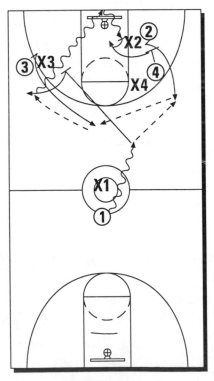

Figure 44: Second Shot

From this point, offensive drills should involve three-on-three play and be extracted directly from a coach's offense. Most shots produced by an offense result from two- or three-player games.

Drilling to develop skills during three-player games can be helpful. The following is an example of such a drill.

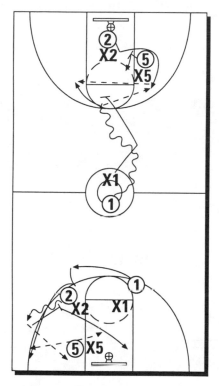

Figure 45: Baseline Screens: Three-on-Three

Baseline Screens: Three-on-Three

Purpose: reading screens, game shots

Player O1 begins beyond half-court with X1 applying pressure. Player O2 begins under the goal, preparing to use O5, who will screen X2.

As O1 moves the ball to the three-point line in the middle lane, O2 sets up his player and uses the screen set by O5. Player O1 then passes the ball to O2, who curls high to the elbow on the way to taking a jump shot.

Once O1 passes the ball to O2, he slides to the weak side elbow in order to stretch the defense in case X1 helps on O2. If X2 and X1 take away the first two options, O5 works for position and receives a pass from O2. Player O5 tries to score as O1 and O2 run a split, creating two more possible options.

Five options become available in this simple play, yet players may only recognize them after they analyze the play.

Chapter 5

A Philosophy of Handling Special Situations

Being effective in responding to special situations can make a positive difference in many games a team plays. Knowing how to respond properly can determine the outcome of games in ways that can affect an entire season.

Because basketball is played at a quick pace with time restraints, a coach must teach his team how to manage the clock, when to foul and when not to foul, who should take certain shots, how to succeed in a game, how to catch up, how to protect a lead, and how to handle other situations. The development of such skills needs constant attention in practice and should be highlighted daily with enough time devoted to these skills.

When the outcome of a game lies in the balance, an aggressive team will succeed most of the time. Thus, in practice, a team must learn to develop aggressiveness and the ability to execute properly in pressure situations, just as it would any other skill. Coaches can also develop their players' confidence by working on various pressure situations in practice.

Although these special situations can occur at any time during a ball game, they become more significant near the end of a game. Therefore, a team must understand the value of managing time-outs.

Strategies for Sideline and Baseline Out-of-Bounds Play

To create the proper balance in a team's performance—the type that gives a team plenty of opportunities to succeed while playing all over the floor—the coach must teach his players how to execute properly from the sidelines and the baselines. His team should know how to do the following:

- Produce three-point shots from the sideline when needed, without using up a time-out
- Score two points off a sideline play, without using up a time-out
- Score one point to win a game, without using up a time-out

- Defend these sideline and baseline plays while protecting a lead
- Use baseline out-of-bounds plays to produce the shots needed to win ball games without calling a time-out
- Use out-of-bounds plays to create four near receivers while protecting a lead and going full-court
- Keep the best foul shooter on the floor while protecting a lead
- Defend these full-court situations when the team is behind
- Know who to foul
- Use a play from the sideline in the backcourt that will produce both a three-point shot and a two-point shot without calling a time-out
- Have a play ready to move the ball inbounds to protect a lead and to defend this particular situation
- Stop the clock—and understand why the team needs to stop the clock

Decision-Making Criteria

Covering the bases around the court can help prepare a team for late-game situations both offensively and defensively. Coaches are responsible for placing their teams in a position to succeed. Players must develop the ability to succeed through teamwork.

Within all out-of-bounds situations, the time remaining becomes significant. Such situations create decision-making opportunities for the coach. For instance, if only 10 seconds remain in a ball game and a team is down by one point and has the ball out in the front court, the coach will have to decide if he wants his players to (1) move the ball in bounds and then run a quick-hitting play, or (2) use an out-of-bounds play to produce a shot that may come too quickly and, thus, give the ball back to the opponent with enough time on the clock to score.

Coaches who have confidence in their defense might decide that the out-of-bounds play is the proper decision. Those who prefer not to give the ball back to their opponents with too much time left might advise their players to move the ball in and execute a play.

Coaching decisions such as these will naturally turn on the strengths of the team. In order to prepare for the inevitable, the coach should practice making decisions—and he should do so by pretending that he does not have the luxury of a time-out in which to discuss the specifics with his players.

Final Game Minutes

Crunch time, the most critical point in a close game, usually occurs within the final five minutes. From a defensive standpoint, the team's philosophy will be determined by the number of points by which a team is down. In playing catch-up defense, coaches may find that being down 10–12 points requires them to create more action with their press or their half-court trap or their double-teaming of the quarter-court zone—or with player-to-player contact.

Whatever the approach, a team must understand clearly what it is that the coach wants. Teaching a team how to succeed offensively is essential, especially teaching it how to exert offensive pressure whenever possible. Knifing through an opponent's press to dunk the ball, or even just lay it in, can be devastating to that team. Therefore, the offense should always maintain an aggressive controlled presence.

With a solid lead late in a game, the objective is to play against the clock. Efficient teamwork creates the foundation for success. A team's top priorities should include using the clock to its advantage, having the proper players take the proper shots, and keeping the board covered.

If they earn an offensive rebound, players should be certain to make their basket. If they can't, another intelligent option is for them to pass the ball to a perimeter player and use up more of the clock. The offense wants to score points with the clock running. The defense wants to stop the clock by forcing free throws.

Having players work on crunch-time situations is an excellent coaching strategy and a great way to finish daily practice. Players enjoy the competitiveness that these situations call for and, as a result, they gain more confidence. The coach's ultimate goal should be to teach his players how to succeed in close ball games.

Working down from five minutes to one minute—and changing the score in the process—is a great technique to use in practice. Coaches who pay close attention can learn a great deal about their players during this activity.

Offensively, the most important position in out-of-bounds situations is that occupied by the player taking the ball out. This player must remain composed, know the location of his receivers, and be able to keep track of the five-second rule. A player or two on each team can usually retrieve loose balls.

Practicing such crunch-time techniques allows players many opportunities to develop the effective skills needed for both offensive situations and defensive situations. As a result, managing substitutions within the rules, as well as being aware of the number of time-outs remaining, becomes much easier because the team and the coach have learned how to prepare for the inevitable.

Free-throw shooting remains an integral part of a team's success in close games. Consequently, in practice, coaches spend time trying to find ways to place pressure on players to shoot free throws. Therefore, placing a team in a simulated special situation requiring free throws works well.

Helping a team to become the best in the league, the state, the nation, or the world is an enormous task for any basketball coach. Working to accomplish this goal, however, is what coaching is all about. Coaches who have commitment and vision know the value of developing the proper balance in their team's performance. They take pride in ensuring that their team is always well coached and well prepared. Developing a philosophy for dealing with special situations, and then putting that philosophy into practice, can contribute significantly to a team's growth and success.

Chapter 6

A Summer Program

Players should be expected to improve their skills over the summer months and throughout the off-season. They improve more quickly, however, when coaches give them a summer program to follow. Doing so is the responsibility of coaches at all levels.

An overview of basketball in the United States reveals that some coaches focus primarily on developing players' skills in two ways: (1) teaching them to dunk the ball and immediately follow up with sort of a dance, and (2) teaching them to follow a successful three-point shot by engaging in a shoulder bump with their teammates. This approach has all but eliminated the players' use of the 15-foot jump shot and their ability to create this shot off the dribble or the catch. What has happened is that many players have become offensive specialists instead of well-rounded players.

Coaches should teach players to develop basic skills in footwork and shooting. Few truly great players possess the ability to know when to move and to create shots while maintaining a well-balanced athletic stance. Within a coach's program for summer and off-season activities, teaching such fundamentals should be a priority.

Throughout my career, I have coached few perimeter players who demonstrate adequate skill in defensive footwork. Players seem to take fakes from side to side rather than up and back. The off-season can be the best time to help players develop proper footwork habits for defensive play.

As a coach, I have used the following program for a number of years. The program developed as a result of my experiences in coaching. This program has proven effective for my players and, ultimately, for my teams.

Ballhandling

As far as their ability to pass and dribble is concerned, most players need plenty of improvement. Ballhandling drills can be analyzed as carry drills in which players learn to carry the basketball around different parts of their body.

Carry Drills

The players should begin each drill in an athletic position with their feet shoulder-width apart and their knees bent. They should perform the drills slowly at first and then as quickly as possible. These carry drills serve as a great warm-up activity.

The players begin by carrying the ball around their head. They then change to carrying the ball around their waist. With their feet shoulder-width apart, they then move the ball to their right leg, between their knee and ankle. They should keep their head up so they can look downcourt.

Next, they move the ball to their left leg and follow that with a figure-eight carry, or one that moves the ball in a figure-eight pattern on their body. Again, they should keep their head up and their eyes looking down the court.

Staying with the figure eight, they should then skip as they carry the ball. Finally, the drill involves a figure-eight carry as they walk forward and backward.

Once the carry drills begin, they should follow the same progression and end with the players doing the figure-eight carry backward drill. The drills take about five minutes total.

Dribbling Drills

Dribbling One Basketball

Players should begin the drill in an athletic stance in which they are properly balanced on both feet with their head up. As they perform these drills using one basketball, they should also keep their opposite hand in a position to offer help or protection while they dribble.

They should first dribble a ball all the way around their right leg, taking care not to push the ball. From their right leg, the ball must be moved to their left leg.

The players should then begin the figure-eight dribble while remaining in a balanced position, keeping their upper body over the ball. They should move to the figure-eight dribble forward and backward drill, keeping their head up while looking down the court.

The ball must remain in the middle of their stance while they alternate dribbles with each hand, first in front of their body and then in back of their body. Dribbles must be made on the floor and inside the players' legs. This drill ends with players using the four-hand dribble while walking forward and backward.

As the players participate in the dribbling drills with one ball, they should maintain a balanced athletic stance. Both their hands should be properly conditioned, and their vision should remain focused down the court. This series of drills takes about 10 minutes.

Dribbling Two Basketballs

Dribbling two balls, one with each hand, serves as an excellent way to strengthen a player's weak hand. The players should perform them after the one-ball drills.

Players should begin while standing properly balanced on both feet. They should initially dribble one ball high and one ball low to develop their concentration. From there, they should alternate the high dribble and the low dribble.

Next, they should practice dribbling each ball up and back on the sides, which is a frequently used dribble. Dribbling while moving each ball from hand to hand in front of them also helps to develop their concentration.

In addition, the players should learn how to take the ball in their right hand and dribble it around their right leg, all the while maintaining their dribble with their left hand. They can help develop the proper skills with their weak hand by taking the ball in their left hand (assuming it is their weak hand) and dribbling it around their left leg while they maintain their dribble with their right hand. From that point, they can further develop their confidence by speed dribbling with two balls to half-court and back.

Dribbling Three Basketballs

Constant drilling should help the players develop confidence in dribbling three balls with two hands. Obviously, this drill requires more concentration than usual, since the players must control three balls at once.

Players begin by holding three balls cradled in their arms. They throw one up in the air to buy time as they start the other two balls. Once they control two balls, players must move to controlling the third ball while continuing to dribble the middle ball. Their goal should be to create a two-bounce rhythm, leaving the outside ball on its own while dribbling the middle ball.

Once the players develop confidence in keeping all three balls going, they can continue the drill. The challenge becomes keeping three balls in proper rhythm and then taking the left ball around their left leg, while keeping the middle ball going and then recovering in time to dribble the free ball while maintaining rhythm. Players with weak left hands find it especially challenging to dribble a ball around their right leg and then return to a three-ball rhythm.

Drills using two and three balls take about 15 minutes each. Conducting the carry drills, in addition to the drills that call for dribbling one, two, and three basketballs, takes about 30 minutes total. Coaches should understand the value of ballhandling drills. These drills help their players to learn to become more skilled with the ball.

Offensive Drills in Change-of-Direction Dribbling and Game Shots

The next set of drills simulates the fast break, while emphasizing change-of-direction dribbling and game-like shots. From the fast break, the drills move to the scoring area, with the emphasis on developing skills in making quick decisions, reading defenses, using change-of-direction dribbling, and footwork shooting. These drills, which can be designed in different ways, are quite effective.

Full-Court Change-of-Direction Dribbling

Purpose: change-of-direction dribbling and finishing the fast-break series

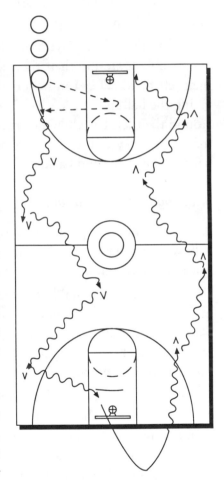

Four cones are placed down the court on one side in a staggered pattern, and four more are placed back up the court on the other side in the same pattern. Players begin on the baseline with a ball. A coach begins in the middle of the lane.

The first player passes the ball to the coach, sprints toward the first cone, and receives a pass back. The player immediately changes direction and heads to the next cone. The player must attack each cone, staying low, and changing direction as quickly as possible. After changing direction at the last cone, the player finishes the play with a specific shot. Each player retrieves the ball and works back up the court on the other side.

As each player passes the first cone, the next player begins. Following four trips up and down the court, the players should take a short break. This break is an excellent time to shoot free throws. After they practice their free-throw shooting, the players should repeat the drill on the left side of the court.

Figure 46: Full-Court Change-of-Direction Dribbling

The In-Between Game

Purpose: making quick decisions, change of direction dribbles, and balanced shots

Depending on the number of players on hand, this series of drills can be conducted from both sides of the court at the same time. If there are only four or fewer players, it is a good idea to focus on one side of the court first and then move to the other side.

Three cones simulating defenders are set up on each side of the court. The coach, who works from the top of the free-throw circle, begins with the ball.

Players prepare to catch a ball and make a quick-decision drive past the first cone, using two dribbles, and then shoot a balanced jump shot over the second cone. Each player becomes responsible for his own ball.

Figure 47: The In-Between Game

Players then repeat this drill on the opposite side. They should continue the drill until the coach becomes satisfied with their progress.

Next, players must make a quick-decision drive past the first cone, change direction at the second cone, and shoot a balanced jump shot over the third cone. Again, the players should repeat the drill on the opposite side until the coach becomes satisfied with their progress.

A final time through the drill, each player should make a quick-decision drive past the first cone, change direction at the second cone, change direction at the third cone, and finish the play with a baby hook shot.

Flare-Game Shooting

Purpose: flare shooting, making quick decisions, and flare series

Cones simulating defenders are placed on the court in such a way that they create a flare screen that requires quick decisions in the middle and baseline areas.

The first player with the ball sets his player up and works off the first cone, flaring to the wing for a jump shot. Next, the player flares to the wing, making quick-decision drives toward the middle cone and shooting the jump shot. Afterward, the player makes quick-decision drives toward the cone on the baseline.

The drill ends with players making quick-decision drives and change-of-direction dribbles, followed by baby hook shots and pull-up jump shots.

Figure 48: Flare-Game Shooting

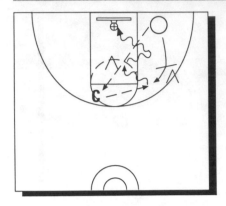

Figure 49: Back-Pick Game

Back-Pick Game

Purpose: back pick, quick decisions, and back-pick series

This drill requires the use of three cones for the back-pick series. The drill begins with the coach passing the ball to a player.

The players try to simulate a back pick (screen) on the first cone and step to catch the pass as they prepare to shoot the jump shot. The second time, they back pick, step to catch, make a quick-decision drive toward the second cone, and shoot a jump shot. The last time through, they make a quick-decision drive following the catch, take a change-of-direction dribble at the second and third cones, and finish with a reverse lay-in or baby hook shot.

Baseline Screening Series (Part 1)

Purpose: footwork shooting, reading screens

This drill requires two cones and two basketballs.

The coach stands at the top of the circle and prepares to pass the ball to a player. One player goes four times in a row, and then the next player follows. They simulate the defense, following the shooter.

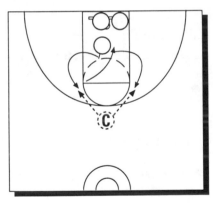

Figure 50: Baseline Screening Series (Part 1)

The player begins under the goal and uses either cone to start the drill. The player moves to the elbow for the jump shot. Next, the player sprints to the area in front of the rim and moves to the opposite side to the elbow.

Players waiting in line become responsible for returning the ball to the coach.

Figure 51: Baseline Screening Series (Part 2, Fade)

Baseline Screening Series (Part 2, Fade)

Purpose: reading screens, footwork shooting

Coaches conduct this drill in the same way as the previous drill. This time, however, players beginning under the rim must bump and fade toward the corner as they take the jump shot. The defense goes over the screen. Again, each player goes four times.

Figure 52: Baseline Screening Series (Part 3)

Baseline Screening Series (Part 3)

Purpose: curls and baby hook shots

This drill requires the use of two cones. The coach begins by passing the ball to a player.

The players who begin under the rim now run a hard curl off the cones, shooting a baby hook shot with their weak hand. All players should develop the proper skill in making this shot.

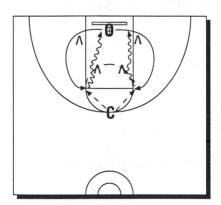

Figure 53: Baseline Screening Series (Part 4)

Baseline Screening Series (Part 4)

Purpose: reading screens, in-between game

This drill requires four cones so players can work on change-of-direction dribbling and well-balanced baby hook shots. The drill begins with the coach passing the ball to a player.

Players who begin under the rim again move to the elbow. On the catch, however, they must make a quick-decision drive at the second cone and use a change-of-direction dribble going into a baby hook shot. Utilizing both sides of the floor once again requires that the players use their weak hand.

***Figure 54: Baseline Screening
Series (Part 5)***

Baseline Screening Series (Part 5)

Purpose: react to defender and footwork
shooting

This drill requires the use of two cones.
The drill begins with the coach passing the
ball to a player.

The player who begins under the rim
again moves to the elbow, simulating the situation of having a defense follow him. This
time on the catch, however, the player must
drop step to the outside, using two or three
dribbles prior to stepping back into a jump
shot.

Using the drop step instead of a pivot
becomes crucial in this drill. The drop step
creates the space necessary to execute the shot,
thus sealing the defender and placing him in
a difficult position.

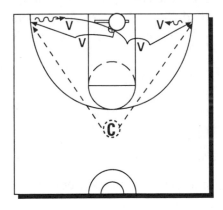

***Figure 55: Baseline Screening
Series (Part 6)***

Baseline Screening Series (Part 6)

Purpose: reading screens, quick decisions,
and footwork shooting

This drill requires four cones placed approximately six feet off the lane line on and
parallel to the baseline. The drill begins with
the coach passing the ball to a player.

Players beginning under the rim must
fade off the first cone toward the corner. On
the catch, they must make a quick-decision
drive toward the second cone, using two
dribbles and then shooting a jump shot. This
drill should help the players develop the ability to make this increasingly difficult shot.

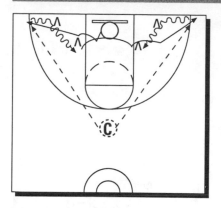

Figure 56: Baseline Screening Series (Part 7)

Baseline Screening Series (Part 7)

Purpose: reading screens, quick decisions, in-between game

This drill again requires four cones placed approximately six feet off the lane line and parallel to the baseline. The coach begins the drill by passing the ball to a player.

The player fades toward the corner. On the catch, the player makes a quick-decision drive toward the second cone, changes direction back to the first cone, and takes a short bank jump shot.

Defensive Drills

The drills mentioned thus far in this chapter have all been offensive-oriented drills that emphasize the development of proper ball skills. Working on defensive skills in the summer, however, remains equally important. For instance, utilizing the spots drill (Chapter 3, Figure 11) can reinforce proper individual footwork skills. (Playing one-on-one remains one of the best ways to improve defensively.)

The spots close outs drill (Chapter 3, Figure 12) is effective, simply because closing out is the most difficult position in which defenders find themselves.

The rotate to close out with help drill (Chapter 3, Figure 14) is effective, too, because it emphasizes closing out into two-on-two. This particular drill can also become quite competitive and, ultimately, invaluable to the players and the team.

Deny and Lead In

Purpose: denial, one-on-one

Player O1, who begins this drill on the wing, must move to free himself from his defender. Player X1 must deny all passes to O1.

The coach begins at the guard position with two basketballs. As the coach throws the ball to O1, X1 must deny the pass by knocking the ball down and keeping it in play.

Player O1 continues to try to become free. X1 must still deny all passes. (Extra players should retrieve the basketballs and return them to the coach.)

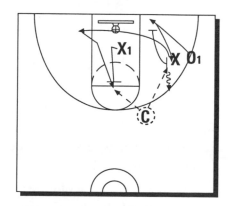

Figure 57: Deny and Lead In

On command, O1 sprints to the weak side. Player X1 must open up, seeing O1 and the coach.

Player O1 then straight cuts to the ball, with X1 denying the pass. Finally, player O1 must become free, allowing the drill to end one-on-one.

Two-on-One Lead-in Rotate

Purpose: denial and rotation

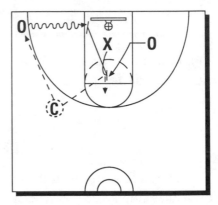

Figure 58: Two-on-One Lead-in Rotate

One offensive player (O1) begins this drill outside the opposite block. The other offensive player (O2) begins in the ball-side corner. The defender (X1) begins in the middle of the lane.

The coach begins on the wing with two basketballs. Player O1 straight cuts to the ball to try to catch it just below the foul line.

The coach throws the first ball to O1 and then immediately throws a second ball to O2. Player X1 must deny the pass to O1 and rotate to take a charge or block the shot of O2.

This drill is effective in helping develop the players' denial skills. They also learn how to rotate properly to prevent a score.

In-Between Game Two-on-One

Purpose: dribbling, two-on-one, and shot blocking

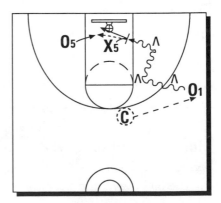

Figure 59: In-Between Game Two-on-One

Three cones simulating defenders are set up on one side of the court in the same way that they are arranged for the in-between game drill (see Figure 47).

Player X5, a shot blocker, begins in the area in front of the rim. Either player O5 or another front-line player begins outside the free-throw lane on the weak side.

The coach throws a pass to O1, who makes a quick-decision drive and two change-of-direction dribbles, ultimately attacking X5. Player X5 tries to do one of the following: block O1's shot, deflect O1's pass to O5, or block O5's shot.

During a summer program, coaches should ultimately require three-on-three play. Doing so is an excellent way to help players learn to improve both their offensive and defensive skills.

Finally, free-throw shooting should become part of a summer program. Players should learn to take advantage of their free throws, because they are easy points. Using proper techniques to throw at least 100 free throws daily can increase players' shooting percentage.

Developing offensive skills involves work that must be done with fundamentals in mind. Players love to play pickup games in the off-season. Coaches should encourage such play. Recommending that players engage in a program of drill activities that allows them to set and achieve new goals may have the added advantage of encouraging players to use their pickup games not only to defeat opponents, but also to improve their skills.

Chapter 7

Continuing Education for Coaches

Coaches should always make their own professional growth a priority. They should not become complacent, regardless of the success they have earned. Rather, they need to keep searching for an advantage. If they do not, another coach in their league will.

Summer Activities

Summer self-improvement projects can serve as wonderful opportunities for growth. Working at summer camps remains one of the best ways to continue learning. Using teaching stations, coaching a team, and sharing ideas with other coaches can all help a coach to develop his skills.

Year-Round Activities

Coaches should also develop the habit of attending game practices at all levels of basketball. High school, college, and professional team practices naturally serve as classrooms for coaches. Attending formal coaching clinics in the local area or elsewhere can be beneficial, as well.

Watching videotapes of one's favorite coach or players can also teach and inspire coaches. I recall watching many tapes of Bill Walton as a college player, for example, in the hopes of developing my coaching and teaching skills with post players. Thanks to advancements in computer technology, such tapes are an efficient way to learn.

Reading basketball books can also be stimulating, whether they are autobiographies, biographies, histories, how-to books, or reference books. One special technique I use is to highlight the best parts of my favorite books and then type up or write out the excerpts. I then place the excerpts in a notebook I keep on the topic of the excerpt.

In addition, planning chalk challenges can promote one's growth. Coaches can use a blackboard to present basketball scenarios to assistants or other coaches. The coach with the chalk must diagram the solution. Some of the greatest arguments I have ever had developed during such activities. Everyone always left the room convinced he had won.

Simply spending time with a pad of paper and a pen, working on X's and O's, can add up to time well spent. Coaches may even surprise themselves with some of the great ideas they can produce by just studying an assortment of defensive and offensive strategies.

Creating notebooks that emphasize various aspects of the game can be extremely beneficial and rewarding. This process can help coaches organize their approach to coaching and identify the coaching topics on which they need more information. They can develop notebooks on such topics as defense, offense, transition, special situations, drills of all kinds, and whatever else seems essential.

Chapter 8

Conclusion

The preservation of the integrity of the game of basketball through personal honesty and responsibility will always be important to players, coaches, and fans. Coaches can best preserve this integrity by developing their own philosophies of the game, as well as their plans to achieve their goals.

My philosophy of basketball developed from my view of the nature of the game and from my learning about coaches' goals and the elements of a balanced approach to coaching. My experience as a high school and college basketball player, as well as a coach of college, international, and NBA teams, helped me to develop my philosophy.

Successful teams have 12 traits. In addition, their coaches have a vision, goals, and an action plan they need in order to maintain their process of team building and achieving success.

Teaching players to succeed in both their defensive and offensive play can be achieved through an understanding of the organization, goals, strategies, and drills that reflect a coach's philosophy.

Coaches must prepare players to handle special situations. They must also help their players to develop and hone their skills through a summer program.

Finally, coaches should make their own continuing education a priority. A life in the game of basketball can be fulfilling if coaches approach it with a high level of integrity and work to become the best they can be. The life lessons learned throughout the experience will be important to their success in basketball and beyond.

Glossary

ASSIST. A pass by an offensive player to a teammate that results in a basket.

ASSIST-TO-TURNOVER RATIO. The percentage of passes that results in the loss of the ball by the opponent.

BACK CUT. An aggressive sprint by an offensive player while reacting to ball denial in order to relieve ball pressure.

BACKDOOR. A type of offensive pick (or screen) play similar to the give-and-go play involving two players, except that it involves one additional player; an offensive player who did not first pass the ball to another teammate becomes free to receive the ball after it is passed between two other players and is able to shoot it.

BACK PICK (SET). When an offensive player sets a screen behind a defender and in front of the basket.

BALANCED SHOT (STRONG POSITION). Maintaining equal weight on both feet while maintaining an athletic position in which the knees are bent and the body is ready to move.

BALL HANDLER. The player with the ball.

BALL PRESSURE. A legal aggressive move made by a defender toward an offensive player with the ball.

BLOCKED SHOT. A defensive play to deflect a shot by the use of a hand or an arm.

BUMP. A defensive tactic used against a screening action to slow down an offensive player.

CENTER. Often the largest, tallest, and strongest player.

CLOSE OUT. When a defender rotates to a receiver to discourage shots or dribbling.

CONTESTS (CONTESTING). A player's moving his hand up around a shooter's wrist, thus creating an adjusted shot, or rotating quickly with his hand up to rush a shot.

COVER A SCREEN. In a shell situation, a player reacts defensively to a screening action.

CROSSOVER. A change-of-direction dribble.

CROSS SCREEN. An offensive play designed to disrupt the path of the defender, set from one block on the free-throw lane of the court near the basket to the block on the opposite side.

CURL. An offensive move involving a circular cut or motion to the basket.

> **HARD CURL.** A tight circular movement.

> **SOFT CURL.** A large circular movement.

CUT (GOAL CUT). An aggressive sprint to the basket.

DEFENSE. The team without the ball.

DEFLECTION. To change the direction of a ball's flight.

DELAY. To slow down; an offensive strategy to use up time, not score, or protect a lead late in a game by passing and dribbling to keep the ball away from the other team.

DENIAL. To keep someone from catching the ball.

DOUBLE-TEAM. Two defensive players guard one offensive player with the ball to try to force a turnover.

DRIBBLE. Bounce the ball.

> **CONTROL DRIBBLE.** A slow, deliberate, protective style of dribbling.

> **SPEED DRIBBLE.** Running fast while dribbling.

DROP STEP. A post move in which a player pivots to the baseline.

DOUBLE-TEAM (TRAP). When two players move to guard a single player on the opposing team who has the ball.

DUNK (SLAM DUNK, JAM). A field goal made by a player's slamming the ball through the basket from above the rim.

ELBOW. The intersection of the foul line and the lane line on the court.

FADE. A reaction to a defender going over the top of a screen.

FAKE. A deceptive movement with any part of the body to confuse or distract defenders.

FAST BREAK (RUN-AND-SHOOT). Following a block, a steal, or a rebound, the offensive team pushes the ball in a quick, organized fashion toward the basket on the opposite side of the court.

FIELD GOAL. A basket worth two points—three points if the player shoots from behind the three-point line.

FIELD-GOAL PERCENTAGE. The number of field goals made, divided by the number attempted.

FLARE SCREEN. An offensive play aimed at the court area at an angle to the outside of a defender's shoulder that is designed to disrupt the path of the defender.

FLASH CUT. A quick sprint by an offensive player from the baseline to the middle of the floor.

FOOT FAKE. Initial stages of a movement with the foot in one direction to deceive the offense into believing one will move in that direction.

FORWARD. A front-line player who is often taller and stronger than both guards, but shorter than the center.

> **SMALL FORWARD.** An agile player who is smaller than the big forward.

> **BIG FORWARD.** A player who is smaller than the largest center.

FREE THROW. An extra shot worth one point that is earned by one team when the other team is penalized for having committed a personal foul.

FREE-THROW PERCENTAGE. The number of free-throw shots made out of those attempted.

FRONTCOURT. The part of the floor that lies ahead of an offensive team as it moves toward the basket. The backcourt is the floor area that its opponent defends.

FULL-COURT PRESS. A movement in which the defensive team in the backcourt extends its players the full length of the court; the goal is to obtain turnovers.

GET A STOP. To obtain the ball without the other team's scoring.

GIVE-AND-GO. When an offensive team player passes the ball to a teammate, runs to the basket, and then returns to get the ball back from the player.

GOAL CUT (STRAIGHT CUT). An aggressive sprint to the basket.

GOALTENDING. A defensive player's illegal touching of the ball on its flight down into the basket. If called on the defense, the shot is scored as a field goal. If called on the offense, the defensive team is awarded possession and no points are scored.

GUARDING. Defensive shadowing of offensive players to prevent their movement toward the basket or toward another player to pass the ball.

GUARDS. Backcourt players who are the shortest and fastest members of a team's five players; they play farther away from the basket than the two forwards and one center. They initiate and direct plays and serve as ball handlers.

> **POINT GUARD.** Assumes major ballhandling responsibilities.

> **SHOOTING GUARD.** The best shooter.

HAND OFF. To give the ball to another teammate by passing it directly.

DRIBBLE HANDOFF. Giving the ball to another teammate after dribbling it first.

HARD FOUL. A deliberate or obvious foul; to take a hard foul means placing oneself in a situation to receive a foul in order to change the nature of the play on the court, especially in the final minutes, to keep the player with the ball from dribbling to the basket.

HELPS. A player rotates below dribble penetration, forcing a pass, or rotates to stop dribble penetration, causing the offensive player either to turn the ball over or take a poor shot.

HOOK SHOT. A shot made by the arm of the front-line player, usually the center, as his arm movements form an arc as he throws the ball into the basket.

> **BABY HOOK SHOT.** Such a shot made closer to the basket than the regular shot, with the arm movement forming a smaller arc.

INBOUND. To put the ball in play from out of bounds.

JUMP SHOT. Throwing the ball into the basket after first jumping straight up into the air and releasing the ball at the peak of the jump.

BANK JUMP SHOT. The same movement created by throwing the ball off the backboard.

KEY AREA. The area that includes the foul circle, the foul lane, and the free-throw line.

LAY-IN. A shooter close to the basket jumps to place the ball on top of the rim to allow it to fall in.

LAYUP. A shooter close to the basket jumps to place the ball against the backboard so that it drop into the basket.

LOOSE BALL. A ball possessed by neither team.

MAN-TO-MAN DEFENSE. When each team member is assigned to guard or defend against a team member from the other team as he moves all over the court.

MATCH UP. To move into position.

MID-COURT. The center line dividing the court in half.

OFFENSIVE. The team that has the ball.

OUTLET PASS. After gaining possession of the ball, a player moves the ball to a perimeter player, who initiates the fast break.

OUT OF BOUNDS. Not in play.

PASS. Throwing the ball to a teammate.

> **BASEBALL PASS.** A one-handed overhand throw.

> **BEHIND-THE-BACK PASS.** Using one hand to move the ball behind the back in the waist area.

> **BOUNCE PASS.** To pass the ball by bouncing it once on the floor to move it away from a defender and to a fellow teammate.

> **CHEST PASS.** Giving the ball to a receiver by using two hands while holding the ball at one's chest.

> **LOB PASS.** A two-handed movement involving throwing the ball high to a receiver who is still moving.

PERIMETER. The court area outside the key.

PICK (SCREEN) OR SETTING A PICK (OR SCREEN). A legal play used by an offensive team member to try to disrupt the movement of a defender guarding the offensive player with the ball; the offensive player stands between his teammate with the ball and that teammate's defender, but he uses no physical contact; the screen moves to the defender and remains stationary; this permits another offensive player to take a shot or move closer to a basket.

PICKED OFF. A successful pick (or screen) play made by the offense against the defense.

PICK-AND-ROLL (OR SCREEN-AND-ROLL). An offensive play in which the player disrupts the movement of the defender while a teammate dribbles the ball to the middle of the floor.

PIVOT. Movement of one foot while keeping the other foot on the floor.

> **INSIDE PIVOT.** Moving one foot to one side of the body or the other, in front of the body.

> **OUTSIDE PIVOT.** Moving one foot to one side of the body or the other, behind the body.

POST. The area including the foul line and the free-throw lane line.

> **LOW POST.** The block-to-block area of the lane line near the basket.

> **HIGH POST.** The elbow-to-elbow area of the lane line near the free-throw line.

POST PLAY. Activity in the post area of the court in which a player acts as a screen for a teammate in the same area.

POSTING UP. When a post player works to catch the ball.

PRESS. Format used by a defensive team to guard opponents all over the court in an attempt to force turnovers; the press can be either a man-to-man or a zone (except that the NBA does not permit the zone).

REBOUND. Either team's attempt to retrieve a ball after a missed shot.

> **DEFENSIVE REBOUND.** Making a shot after it was first unsuccessfully attempted by a member of the opposing team.

> **OFFENSIVE REBOUND.** Making a shot after it was first unsuccessfully attempted by a teammate with the ball.

RUN-AND-JUMP. A play in which a defender runs to the ball, and the defender on the ball rotates to the next open player.

RUN-AND-TRAP. A play in which the defender runs at the player with the ball while the defender of the player with the ball stays in place so that together they can trap their opponent.

SCREEN (SEE PICK).

SHELL (SHELLING). A drill that helps to develop certain defensive techniques.

SHOT CLOCK. The timing device that begins as soon as a team takes possession of the ball.

SHOT FAKE. Initial stages of a movement with either the hands, the arms, the head, or any other part of the body in one direction that is intended to deceive the offense into believing the players is going to shoot in a particular direction.

SIXTH PLAYER. The first substitute who will be used.

SPOTTED UP. The floor area from where players prepare to shoot.

SQUARE UP. To stand with one's shoulders facing the basket.

STEAL. To take the ball away from a player on the opposite team.

STRAIGHT CUT (SEE GOAL CUT).

STRAIGHT MAN. Man-to-man defense.

STRONG SIDE OF THE COURT. The half of the court in which the ball is being played.

TEAM. Two forwards, two guards, and one center.

TEN-SECOND RULE. The requirement regarding the amount of time one can remain in the backcourt before having to move the ball across the mid-court line.

TIP-IN. A field goal occurring close to the basket that is made by a member of the same team or the opposing team by using the fingers of the hand to move the ball into the properly aimed position in its flight.

TRANSITION (TRANSITION GAME). The conversion of play from one end of the court to the other.

TRAP (SEE DOUBLE-TEAM).

TRIPLE-THREAT. Maintaining a balanced athletic stance, with knees bent and body ready to move, before shooting, passing, or dribbling the ball.

TURNOVER. The loss of the ball by the offensive team to its opponent before the offensive team has a chance to try for a basket.

WEAK HAND. The hand not usually used by the player.

WEAK SIDE OF THE COURT. The side of the court on which the ball is not being played.

ZONE. A defensive play in which all five players are assigned specific areas of the court to guard.

About the Author

Bob Hill is a basketball broadcast journalist, consultant, writer, and speaker.

He played both basketball and baseball at Worthington High School in Worthington, Ohio. He also played basketball and baseball at Bowling Green State University in Bowling Green, Ohio, where he completed his B.S. in secondary education in 1971.

After serving briefly with the San Diego Padres' baseball team in the summer of 1971, Mr. Hill was hired as an assistant basketball coach at Bowling Green State University. There he also earned his M.Ed. in secondary education in 1972.

He served as an assistant basketball coach at the University of Pittsburgh in Pittsburgh, Pennsylvania from 1975 to 1977 and at and the University of Kansas in Lawrence from 1977 to 1985.

Mr. Hill worked as an assistant basketball coach for the New York Knickerbockers (Knicks) of the National Basketball Association (NBA) in 1985 and 1986 and head coach from 1986 to 1987.

He began his career in basketball broadcast journalism while working for the University of Kansas, as well as the Sports Channel in New York City, in 1987 and 1988.

Between 1987 and 1988, he served as head coach of the Topeka Sizzlers of the Continental Basketball Association and scout for the Charlotte Hornets, an NBA team.

From 1988 to 1989, he was head coach of the Virtus Knorr team of the Italian Professional basketball league.

Mr. Hill returned to the NBA, serving the Indiana Pacers as an assistant coach from 1989 to 1990 and head coach from 1990 to 1993. He then served the Orlando Magic as an assistant coach from 1993 to 1994 and the San Antonio Spurs as head coach from 1994 to 1997.

Since 1996, he has served as head coach for the Pro Development Camp, an annual six-day summer camp established by Frank Martin and Bill Walton for NBA and college basketball players.

He has worked since 1997 as a consultant for the New Jersey Nets, an NBA team.

Since 1997, Mr. Hill has been a broadcast journalist providing color commentary and studio analysis for NBA games for several national television networks. These include the Entertainment and Sports Programming Network (ESPN), the Cable News Network Sports Illustrated channel (CNNSI), Turner Network Broadcasting (TNT), and The Sports Network (TSN) (the Canadian equivalent of ESPN).

He resides in San Antonio, Texas.